DIALOGUES WITH
THE HOLY SPIRIT

In an unrelenting symphony of love, joy, and peace,
The Creator calls us home and teaches the way.

Dialogues with the Holy Spirit

journal of a student

A concrete approach to turning the battleground into the playground where joy, laughter, and peace beyond your current understanding are waiting.

Rusty Stephens, *scribe*

BALBOA.
PRESS
A DIVISION OF HAY HOUSE

Balboa Press books may be ordered through booksellers or by contacting:

Balboa Press
A Division of Hay House
1663 Liberty Drive
Bloomington, IN 47403
www.balboapress.com
1-(877) 407-4847

Because of the dynamic nature of the Internet, any web addresses or
links contained in this book may have changed since publication and
may no longer be valid. The views expressed in this work are solely those
of the author and do not necessarily reflect the views of the publisher,
and the publisher hereby disclaims any responsibility for them.

The author of this book does not dispense medical advice or prescribe
the use of any technique as a form of treatment for physical, emotional,
or medical problems without the advice of a physician, either directly
or indirectly. The intent of the author is only to offer information
of a general nature to help you in your quest for emotional and
spiritual well-being. In the event you use any of the information in
this book for yourself, which is your constitutional right, the author
and the publisher assume no responsibility for your actions.

ISBN: 978-1-4525-3687-3 (sc)
ISBN: 978-1-4525-3688-0 (eb)
ISBN: 978-1-4525-3689-7 (hc)

Library of Congress Control Number: 2011912040

Printed in the United States of America
Balboa Press rev. date: 10/31/2011

A human being is part of a whole, called by us the Universe, a part limited in time and space. He experiences himself, his thoughts and feelings, as something separated from the rest a kind of optical delusion of his consciousness. This delusion is a kind of prison for us, restricting us to our personal desires and to affection for a few persons nearest us. Our task must be to free ourselves from this prison by widening our circles of compassion to embrace all living creatures and the whole of nature in its beauty.

Albert Einstein

Contents

Introduction   ix

PART 1   HOW TO SEE   1
PART 2   OF THE ESSENCE   19
PART 3   OF FAITH AND FLIGHT   31
PART 4   THE GREATER ONE   37
PART 5   BE IN THE WORLD BUT NOT OF IT   57
PART 6   WE ARE ONE, EVER   77
PART 7   HONESTY OF MIND, SINCERITY OF SPIRIT,
         AND DETACHMENT   92
PART 8   THE MASTERS OF WISDOM   107
PART 9   MEDITATE, STUDY, SERVE   128
PART 10 THE LAW OF INVOCATION   143
PART 11 THOUGHTS ARE TRULY THINGS   161
PART 12 FOLLOW YOUR BLISS   169
PART 13 KARMA   181
PART 14 EMERGENCE OF THE WORLD TEACHER   193
PART 15 CROWN THY GOOD   197
PART 16 DOOMSDAY NOT   212
PART 17 THE HOLY SPIRIT   228
PART 18 THE EGO AND COINCIDENCE NOT   258
PART 19 PART-TO-WHOLE   268
PART 20 THE WORK   281
PART 21 FORGIVENESS   295

SOURCES   309
LIST OF EXERCISES   313
END NOTES   315
ON THE COVER   317

DIALOGUES WITH THE HOLY SPIRIT

journal of a student

Introduction

I had for some time been looking for a way to hear, see, touch, feel, and otherwise sense, a new level of understanding about things Spiritual. Whatever was, was no longer working. I had come to the point that I recognized myself as a student but at the same time I was wondering and wandering in my seeking to learn.

The pathways and encounters that had brought me to this realization were many over the past several years and included a rising and recurrent thought. I had been initially successful at ignoring this thought especially early on and sometimes for years at a time. But there it was again and again recurring with greater frequency and a little louder each time. The thought was and remains an awareness from somewhere that keeps telling me, ever so softly but ever so persistently, there is more, there is higher stuff, there is greater knowledge, and it is yours to seek when you are ready.

In addition to that thought, which I finally came to accept as something I must deal with, there were also during this time a series of disturbing events connected to relationships. I had come to recognize a pattern in my interactions with several people over many years. These were people who were important to me. The pattern was such that each person in their own way was at first a respected and often dear brother or sister only to have a point come when the interaction with them became difficult, frustrating, and fearful. I had tried everything I knew, including relocating and changing jobs, to get away from very unpleasant people. However, no matter how I tried to treat them differently and/or run away, they kept coming into my life. The names and faces would change but the interpersonal issues were the same and I was finding them to be destructive.

I reached a point where I simply had to have a better way. I also reached a point where it was beginning to dawn on me that I was part and parcel of both the problem and solution. Having no real sense of what that meant, only a growing sense that hurt, harm and hate were not what I wanted to receive and give, I began reading every book that seemed to hold the possibility of providing answers. This included a few that literally fell at my feet along with some others that showed up in my life in such a way as to be equally demanding of my attention.

Those readings led me to begin meditation. Meditation was done first as a coping method for stress and I fairly quickly saw results. However, meditation soon led to a series of impressions, mental images, and opening of other levels of both understandings and many more questions. That set of experiences plus the things I was reading, led me to think I was making some progress. However, after a while that sense of progress was given over to an increasing level of frustration as I reached a point where no progress was evident, what little clarity I had seemed to have vanished. I felt as though I was wandering in a wilderness not of my own making and I was increasingly more desperate to reach some understanding. The need to make sense of all of this on again, off again knowing and not knowing had become no longer an option to be taken up someday. The need had become pressing. I could not seem to do anything with it and I could no longer ignore it nor let it go. It was like hearing a distant call but it was coming from me.

There was at once and at the same time the feeling that I was at a point where I knew less and less while having the tantalizing impression that somewhere just on the periphery of my vision was meaning, confirmation, validation, a vast new field of knowing, laughter, joy, and great Love. Reinforcement was also coming to me in dreams, a line from a movie, a snatch of dialogue between strangers as I passed them, clouds, music, the flight of birds, sudden knowings, and the grand sweep of a clear night sky. I would be moved and inspired by writings I would find from the great minds of history as well as soup can labels. I was no longer surprised at such happenings and their accompanying tears, laughter, and moments of great joy. And, this is important as I look back on it; occasionally I could get to a place where I could exclaim aloud "Oh My God!" as I would stand under a canopy of stars overwhelmed with a sense of stunning, awestruck awareness of the holiness, vastness, and pure beauty of the Creator's great cathedral. These moments sustained me and I know now were doorways that were being shown to me. And, they had become the most natural thing in the world.

However, upon awakening or returning mentally to what I considered my more normal frame of mind and routine of daily activities, it was also the most natural thing in the world for it to be like these moments had never happened. Buried and forgotten for days and weeks they would surface again, more and more like both an old ache and an old friend, and would let me see again the potential that I longed to realize and the painful awareness that again and again, and most of the time, the world had taken my attention and that once more I had bought into all that it seemed to be. Indeed vacillation became a major theme of the dialogue and teachings that are chronicled in this *journal of a student*. As this happened over and over and over again, I came to see that I am very attached to the version of the world that is presented by the senses and by my lack of real understanding. I also found that I was afraid.

Then something I could not ignore nor easily forget, what I call a Spiritual fixation, appeared. I had known and written off coincidence before but this, as I watched first with amusement then amazement, and then even some irritation, became simply ridiculous. A pattern appeared and repeated and repeated. I kept encountering the words of the great and probably over-quoted first lines of the introduction by Charles Dickens to <u>A Tale of Two Cities</u>: "It was the best of times, it was the worst of times . . ." It began to bug me as the exact words kept showing up on billboards, my ongoing efforts at study, headlines, conversations, bathroom walls, advertisements, and emails. Over and over and over many days then weeks, I was treated with all manner of shape and form of this refrain. Even then I also knew somehow that I would need to come back to it and now years later, I see that time has come. I use it here because it captures better than anything I could write the nature of that particular point in my life. I also use it by way of defining this time and place on my path because I am now told that there are many of us who are at this point at this time.

Beyond those famous first lines there are several more which illustrate more depthfully where I was when the events that led to this journal came about:

From: <u>A Tale of Two Cities</u>
By Charles Dickens
It was the best of times,
it was the worst of times,
it was the age of wisdom,
it was the age of foolishness,
it was the epoch of belief,
it was the epic of incredulity,
it was a season of Light,
it was the season of Darkness,
it was the spring of hope,
it was the winter of despair,
we had everything before us,
we had nothing before us,
we were all going direct to Heaven,
we were all going direct the other way . . .

So, that is where I had come in my search. I did not know whether to wind my watch or go bowling. I was stuck between all of the poles that Dickens so wonderfully identified plus a few thousand more. I could not see how to go forward and, in moments of clarity, I knew I did not want to go on the way I was going or, God help me, go back. I did know, however, that it meant more and more to me to seek a way forward. Indeed if I now knew anything at all it was that somehow, forward was the only option. I also felt as though I was not moving.

It was then that I hit upon a coping strategy. I got angry. In my anger I spoke directly to God. I made what was a simple but, and I would soon learn, important, clear statement of the problem and, in my relative state of pissed-offedness, my expectation of an answer.

I told God that I had been trying to see, sense and otherwise know the greater thing and my way to it. I also told God of my many efforts including study of a wide range of religions, concepts, philosophies, efforts at prayer, efforts at meditation, and efforts at ignoring the whole thing. I said out loud that I was sick and tired and that as far as I was concerned a Creator who supposedly gave us such a wonderful set of five senses and then refused to use them to communicate with us was not my version of a Creator that I neither could nor wanted to pursue any longer. I said out loud "I am tired of trying to read signs, clouds, chicken entrails, and tea leaves. There must somewhere be a giant red phone with a giant capital letter 'G' on the dial plate and *I want, by God, the 800 number!*" I went on to specify that I wanted that number so I could make calls and I also wanted to get a call. I wanted nothing less than to hear a voice in my head, in English, no tongues please. I also ordered that conversation to be clear, unambiguous, unmistakable, reliable, validatable, and I wanted it now.

I would like to tell you that the sky opened and a ray of light or a dove or at least crap from a bird landed on me and somehow I got the 800 number. It did not work that way but it did work as the beginning. The turning of the corner had come for me in that moment of real frustration and even though angry, genuine prayer.

What came next was a series of very clear, very different, and very weird experiences that were so captivating and telling that I could not any longer just look away and write them off as coincidence, delusion, indigestion, or even swamp gas. The experiences of the birth of babies and the death of loved ones were shown to me to be of equal sacredness and in their own way, miracles. They included a sudden knowing about an issue or a problem that gave me, in an instant, all facts, all questions, all answers, all past, all present and all future possibilities, leaving me with years of work and knowing that I could choose to do it or not. They would to this day include light and electrical phenomena such as street lights going on and off at any time of the day or night when I would pass under them. I know now it was a period of readying me to receive the thing for which I had asked.

Then one night the spiritual phone rang. Looking back on it I now understand that it had been ringing for some time. However, I was trying so hard to hear it only in the narrow way that I had declared that I would actually accept delivery, that I could not see the phone to know it was already there and ringing.

When it came, it was the most simple and natural thing in the world. It came in the form of a conversation. As it began I also was given to know (that is the only way I can with simplicity and honesty describe it—it just came into my mind as a knowing) that for me, the best way to hold up my end, was to write it down as it came. I was awakened at around 3:30 a.m. by the ringing of this spiritual phone. It was clear that this was in response to my asking. I just "knew" it and with it came a very strong impression that I needed to get up and get a pad and a pen. This I did.

What follows is the journal that I kept. It is a *journal of a student*, because it has confirmed that I am a student, as are you and all who have come to this thing we call life. The journaling started out rough and I have left in those first awkward sessions. Also preserved are the often archaic words, grammar, and syntax, along with specific capitalizations. I was to learn that these have a purpose to draw attention and to demonstrate ways of seeing what might be common concepts in new ways. As I gained comfort with the idea and process a somewhat smoother dialogue emerged. However, it remains a journal of conversations and not a transcript. I consider myself to be the *scribe* and not the author.

While editorial attempts have been made to effect smooth transitions, that has not always happened and reflects my own non-linear relationship to the process. I would like to report that it was a well-ordered unfolding. It was not. There were fits and starts, lapses and laziness, and many, many breaks for, in some cases, weeks and occasionally months, at a time.

There are also visits and revisits to certain topics. I came to understand this had to do with my own learning process and that what appeared early on as repetition was seen over time as iteration with each adding more depth of understanding as progressive layers of information and knowing were given. The sequence has been preserved. As a gesture toward making the content flow, this journal has been segmented into numbered parts with a brief subheading for each part. The parts and subheadings are not, however, subject or concept groupings. Most often, more than one concept and/or subject is contained in each part.

Editing was done for a few personal items and to disguise references to persons who helped and were, thank you all, vehicles for teaching me along the way.

From the beginning, I was encouraged to ask questions. At times whether I asked or not I was given guidance on next issues and topics. Some journaling sessions would see only a few sentences and others would see many pages. At times, new sessions would continue on a theme already under development and take up at what was the next sentence or paragraph. At times, especially as I became more acclimated to the process, we would begin with the answer to a question that was only in my mind and before I could articulate it. At times it seemed as though we took up in mid-sentence.

There was nothing at the time at all strange about my conversation partner knowing everything about me and all of us. This included every thought I ever had. So, I did not, early on, think anything about references to events of my day, my thoughts of the day before or many years before, or of the world past or present. Now, however, looking back, I realize that many of these references would appear oblique to a reader. In an effort to make better sense of them I have added detail to questions and/or comments. Otherwise, the content, as much as I have been able to accomplish, is unedited.

I make no claims in effort to encourage acceptance on the part of any who may have this work cross their path. Indeed, if you read this work, you will soon see that I was given to understand that the only test is whether or not it works for you and that there can be no other basis of authenticity, rightness, wrongness, inspiration, or lack thereof for anything found here.

Further, I am to advise you that if you have any sense there may be some truth for you here, then you may wish to consider giving your energy in the form of your attention by reading 50 or so pages. If the content has not spoken to you in some way or rings unclear or untrue for you, put it down and move on. It is not for you at this time.

Lastly, for those for whom these words may find a positive resonance, I am instructed to note that when used the words *"you"* and *"your"*, except where clearly delineated otherwise, are always meant to be in the plural.

The words from the voice that came in response to my call appear indented. Where an exact or very near quote from a known source has been used, an effort to cite (see end notes) the source has been made.

PART ONE

HOW TO SEE

So, I put my pen to paper and a clear voice speaking in English said:

> Being a discourse upon the way of remembering who and what you are, on rejoining what you never left and reframing your view to move you away from the battleground of the present day to the playground of the Soul. Being a concrete approach to turning the battleground into the playground where joy, laughter, and peace beyond your current understanding are waiting.

I was then given the first of what would turn out to be 12 exercises.

EXERCISE 1

HOW TO SEE

The physical eyes do not see the world as it is but as the little ego has conceptualized it. The image in the eye is of a vision that exists in the lower mind before the eye is opened upon the world. Hence the eye does not actually see anything that is real.

Given then that you do not see the real world how do you reorient your looking? How do you learn to see with the eye of the Soul?

First close your physical eyes, draw a deeper than usual breath and calm your lower mind. Then ask for a new prescription to be fitted so as to correct your sight. See this actually happening. See a pair of glasses or contacts being placed into position. See them as shiny crystal and the clearest optics you have ever imagined. Know that when in place they will give you a new clarity of vision that you have never seen before with your waking sight. Know that this new capacity for sight will open unto you the view of joy and love that is a natural part of your looking to your brother as yourself.

Do this exercise every day. Do it anytime you realize that you are looking through only the physical eye. With practice you will be able to use this moment to refocus, to think again, to become centered and connected again, and to thus assert your higher-self. It can be done quickly within the time it takes to draw a deep breath.

Learn to do this when confronted with anything that empowers the little ego. Do this before you respond in thought, word or deed to your brother in any way.

After some practice, this will become easier and you will find that it is no longer a required conscious act but has become a constant and a good habit. This will be a strong start to your reorienting your entire being to the light of your Soul. It is a good first step to a new way of looking at your brother, yourself, and the essential unity of all things.

After working on this exercise there was a pause. I was given to understand that I could ask a question. The question that I formed came from my studies at the time where I had been introduced to the concept of attachment and a new concept, detachment. Thus began the dialogue reported in this *journal of a student.*

What do I do to be free of the attachment and fear?

> Your question really is one of how can I learn and grow in my knowledge, understanding and practice of Spiritual growth. In so declaring, you are stating and showing your readiness for growth and are tapping into the law that is behind the saying "Ask and you shall receive."
>
> The basic answer is that there are three ways to learn and grow Spiritually. They are study, meditate and serve. They go together. Service is the most fruitful of the three because it in reality embodies the other two. More on that later.
>
> To answer your more specific question though and for you personally at this time—write.
>
> Write and leave it to Me. Let go and let your faith take you higher. Do the work as you have seen. Ask for help. It will not be withheld. Do not worry so. Do not sweat.

Much of my motive here is what has been referred to as the dark night of the Soul. I think I have been there much of late and relate it in particular to a brother with whom I am having conflict after a period of being, I thought, on our way to a real and deep friendship. This brother has become increasingly attacking. This relationship has become a very real source of pain for me. What do I do? There has to be a better way.

> You are overreacting. All will be well. You are to learn to handle this kind of energy. I will be with you. I am showing you energy that you must release. Not just for you but for all. It is the energy of fear. Learn to let it go.
>
> Call down the light and have it cleanse you and all others. You know how to do this. Now learn to remember, recall and use it at will.
>
> Stay connected always, not just at high moments.
>
> Take care of your physical needs as well.
>
> Stay on the diet. Get more help. You are feeling better.
>
> Your brother, too, after a period of turmoil, is better. You are My gift to him and him to you.

Okay, I have been trying to call down the light and to remember to use it to cleanse my brother and me. However, I am still very susceptible to the difficulty of the interactions in the relationship. You say to "Learn to let it go." This is easier said than done.

> You do not release it, the energy of fear, because you do not trust. Your faith is hampered by doubt.
>
> Love is letting go of fear. It is truly said that perfect love will cast out fear.

Just remember.

I read in <u>A Course In Miracles</u> of the lesson of specialness which as I understand it is the way that my ego wants me to see the world. That is from a point of being special in my being separate, hurt, not deserving, deserving, etc. Events of the past few days have seemed to remind me of this. It is as if I read something in <u>A Course In Miracles</u> or one of the other books I am working in and then can see it soon unfold in front of me.

> Again, a reference to some study you are doing and have been doing for a while now. It is a good thing.

> Special and specialness are terms we will use often and they refer to any form of thought that holds you as separate from Creation, God, and your brother. So specialness has to do with relationships. Thoughts which commonly indicate a perception on your part or that of a brother or sister of being separate or special include: fear, attack, superiority, inferiority, guilt, unworthiness, hostility, punishment, pain, incompleteness, hate, harm, hurt, emotional debt (either owed to you or by you), anger, indignation, and sin sense.

> You are beginning to see the workings of the classroom you are in. And you have indeed been given opportunity to see the lesson of specialness. You have seen it in your brother and in yourself. Now learn and practice it, this lesson of specialness, every day. Do not see the body. See only Christ for that is all that is there. That is your holy instant. Make it child's play. Play in Me. Laugh, dance,

sing, and play. Transform the battleground into the playground.

Another attack from the brother has occurred and it precipitated a strong reaction of fear in me. However, during the fear episode I was able at least for a few minutes to try and recognize it but, did not seem to have much success. I had known that the meeting would occur and had expected a different outcome.

The field of fear was strong. You are sensitive to it in others as part of your learning to recognize it and deal with it in yourself. Not everyone is so sensitive. It varies with many factors in each person. You are growing more sensitive to it and can use this awareness as a point of knowing with which to trigger your deliberate and conscious seeing of the path of higher consciousness as well as the impetus, the need, to grow onto and into that path. The lessons will come because you have asked for them. They will come because you are ready for them. They will come so as to teach you how to then teach others the way out of their own fear.

These lessons are your own seeing of the two faces of Shiva. As you have often shared with others, the Hindu God Shiva is of two countenances, the destroyer and the restorer. Following the fearsome face of the destroyer is seen the benevolent or angel face of the restorer. Destruction of old forms is necessary to progress on the Spiritual path. New wine must have new bottles.

Given that it did not go as you expected, you can see the need to let go of preconception of what's to come.

Your insight into what and how to treat and learn from your brother's sense of specialness and the behavior that manifests from that sense is but your own such behavior being reflected back to you.

You were given to first love your brother, this brother especially, so that when the rejection came you could respond with that knowledge of that love already in your heart and thus start from the perspective of such love. This you have not done in the past when you have reacted from specialness in other relationships and the result was attack by you as you made what the little ego justifies as a rational self-defense. This is in reality an attack; hence your conflict. It is from the old response pattern. Learn the new. Learn this now. It will move you far.

There is a temple you must enter with your brother. His companionship and unity with you is your key. It is a package deal.

You are blocked. Your instrument needs rest. Rest is not something that you take off and do. It is something that you do moment to moment in the light of your Soul. You get rest by detachment. You rest even in the storm because you can see that there is no storm. You do not need struggle or defense and all the effort that implies because you know there is only the peace of God. You literally come to rest there and with that perspective you are not ever unrested unless you have become unseated. If so, peace, the natural state of the Soul in which rest is the natural result, will have been wrested from you.

How much of my discomfort was diet related?

You have come far in recognizing this connection and are encouraged to continue your discipline in this area. Some of your discomfort was so related in that your physical vehicle can respond better to your higher direction when it is in better shape and better fueled.

However, you must recognize that the battle between the personality (little ego) and the Soul is joined. Indeed, this is the point of this journal.

It is this battle that characterizes most of humanity today and is reflected on the Earth as conflict at all levels that appears every day to grow more ubiquitous and disturbing to more of you. Indeed, it is in its becoming more disturbing to more and more of you that there exists the hope and promise of the great awakening. It is this threshold which is seen by the little ego as storm tossed and increasingly frightening and that you have arrived at as a developing humanity. Thus, the very elements are in chaos because they reflect your connectedness to the lower Kingdoms and thus, is the battle joined.

This is the life to make much progress on surrender to your Soul.

This writing and others to follow will be a byproduct of this tug of war; hence, the need to detach and not care. You can't lose what is not real. Your fear of loss is that of the lower recognizing that it's being called to surrender and give up its specialness.

You do not yet see or really know—even though some taste has been given—what you gain, what you already are. When you know and allow yourself to let go into the light of your Soul, you will wonder why you ever had any fear. You will find the very peace that your personality now only thinks it has but in reality can never have as it is based on the dream/illusion of separateness.

The shortest way is through truth, the easiest way is to see the battleground no longer. See the playground. Play, step into the flow. Be the flow. You are the flow. Teach this and be free.

I now seem to be past a period of turmoil and am trying to see this time and its events in this new perspective.

"See" is the operative word. It is how you see that determines your world and your progress.

Given that you are more centered again, it is appropriate that you ask for information and guidance.

Why can I not just do it? Just take it all in one step and be done?

You can.

Trust.

Continue to respect the law of silence. It is this law that says that you must first do no harm in thought, word or deed. You are tempted to speak of things very personally Spiritual at the early stage of this dialogue and in doing so could actually create difficulty for some around you who are not yet ready.

Some time ago, following a Spiritually tumultuous period when I began to get the idea of finally asking, demanding to hear Your voice, a brother helped with some ideas he said were to give me guidance. They involved what he said was my power to empower which I know now all of us have. It also involved finding and connecting to my group. This was very powerful for me at the time and led to my being open to Your voice when I asked for the 800 number.

Who are/is my group? Will this be a new field of service? How can I get in touch with the power to empower and use it constructively? This memory has come to me also after a very difficult couple of weeks where attacks by the once very trusted brother have put me way off center again and into fear.

> You already are in touch with the power. Keep on. To do so consciously is the goal. Stay connected.
>
> The fear and worry of the last two weeks is and has been a lesson. It was part nutrition and body issues.
>
> See in your brother only Christ. See in yourself only Christ.

The group will come. You will be ready. I will be with you. Take your learning steps now so that when the time comes you too will be ready.

I also realize that this has been such an easy natural thing, this just being with you and talking with you, that it has only now occurred to me to ask for more specifics about who or what you are. How is it that this is happening and is possible?

I have been waiting for you to ask and thought you never would. I am with you always. I am here always. Your Holy Spirit, your very Self, the one that you already are and you may speak to Me at any moment and hear Me at any time. You have only to ask. I am your boon companion who never sleeps but is there. Do not think there are gaps in My being with you—only in your ability to stay connected.

Ever and always and now, I am with you. Take comfort in that. Yes, the Master has touched you and will again. Your Master may come and go as needed and His wisdom requires, but His focus elsewhere does not mean that I am not here. The vehicle, the framework, the mechanism for that contact is through Me, your own personal Holy Spirit. And I am of the same for all your brothers and sisters. They too have a personal Holy Spirit and We are One.

"You can talk to God and listen to the casual reply."[1]

I tell you this. All will yet be well. Go and be blessed for I go with you always, even unto the ends of the

Earth. Even unto the end and beyond this physical body. It is I whom you meet at the end of the tunnel of light. We will hug as before and as we can now do any day at any time. Just ask. Also know that to love your brother to reach out to him in any way is to reach out to Me. We are One.

You have new directions—stay with them. You have been told to laugh. Let it out. You have seen it in others. Appreciate it also in yourself.

You must grow into your power so that you will be able to teach others. You are preparing your instrument which means all of your bodies, vehicles, to work with power and to be prepared to wield it with love and wisdom. You must be able to handle the energy before you can wield it.

Stay the course.

See yourself laughing not only because it is Friday. See yourself laughing because it will be Monday and Tuesday with each a new day and each a miracle to play in. Have the Joy of knowing that your real assignment is to have Joy.

Trust your intuition. Trust Me. Your faith will flow from that.

How to stay connected?

Have Joy. You have felt and seen this possibility— that no matter what, it should be received and responded to as Joy. Cultivate a total context view that nothing fits that is not Joy producing and Joy sustaining.

Yes, you hold the key to making your relationships be of Love and Joy.

You also hold the key that will allow you to send forth the word.

How do I send forth the word?

It will come. This work and other work to follow will be part of it. You will be discovered by those for whom it is appropriate. First you must learn to work with the energy, to see and validate first in your heart of love/wisdom the Christ in everyone, then to positively share by empowering them with the power to empower.

Your brother's recent attack, as is all attack, was a call for help. It was an appeal to share your calm and love/wisdom. There is some remorse now on his part.

See the Christ. See the Christ. All else is illusion of the lower ego.

Nothing can harm you. Teach and know this.

I am your Holy Spirit. It is Me that you talk with. There is a temple you must enter. It is the holy place where you and your brother meet and know each other as in Christ and recognize that in each other. This becomes the holy place and you get there through the miracle moment, the atonement is thus remembered. Anytime, anywhere that you choose to remember, you connect and this is the entrance to the temple.

I have a meeting set for next week with the brother who can be so very difficult. What do I do?

> Your lesson here is clear. In anticipation of the meeting you must only remember and see the divinity in your brother. Call for, ask for, expect—you have a right to—My help. Remember to re-member and do not let—discipline your vehicles—any part give in to fear.

> Expect it to go right and to produce joy. Do not expect anything else. Do not expect a specific ego level outcome.

> Do not cover your bases with others. Seeking support for and validation of your position is of the lower. You don't need it unless you are defending from attack in which case you are seeing your brother as capable of attack. This is not so. The understanding of this will be your salvation from fear.

> All will be well.

> Rest your body. Continue to improve your care for your body. However, you are in charge, not it. It is not who you are. Strike a balance between maintenance and proper attention without either ignoring your body or giving it too much attention. You have a good body. It will serve you well. No body is a good master, however.

My mother's illness grows daily.

> Your mother will be fine. You already know where she is. Love her as you were told. Go to her when

you can. She is moving out and holds on because of fear. She also loves you greatly and always has.

Do not neglect her. Give her full attention and love when you can.

Remember that by doing your own work of awareness and growth you actually speed more the day when you can help others much more and more directly than by worrying now about how to "help" by which the ego means intervene on the material level. Continue the work. Learn to discipline your own vehicles so that they may be better prepared to serve.

How do I discipline my vehicles?

Talk to them. Tell them they are expected to behave as one with you in Christ. Tell them that the days of specialness are over and that you all will now go the way of Oneness with Me, your Soul, your Master, and The Christ. Tell them that it is your will. Create the expectation.

What vehicles?

They are those that make up your presence in the material world. For now understand them to be your body, mind and Spirit. It is at the level of body and mind, especially what is called lower mind, that integration is needed. It is at these levels from whence the fear comes. It is the fear of loss of specialness and fear of surrender to true Joy because of the mistaken belief that separation is actually possible along with the mistaken belief that what is created by the illusion of separation is preferable to the bliss of knowing and living moment to moment in the unity of Christ in all things.

Protect the truth. The shortest way through is the truth. Balance with compassion. Do not second guess; that is a fearful response. Man is the only animal that consciously requires that conflict end in death.

Possess, claim and demonstrate the Joy you are. This will make it real to you and others. Be reminded that your light is for all. To have it in your mind, to know of and understand that it is—is to share it. It is to create the very thought of the possibility for others in their minds that you take and give the light. Let it shine on all others. The very presence in you of this awareness allows for and creates it in your brother. This is how you awaken him. To know this for you and by you first is only the narrow initial step. To possess the knowledge and to manifest its possession sets it into the field so that your brother will also by this exposure, become able, inspired, and knowledgeable.

One must first know that they don't know. So complete is the illusion of specialness that it precludes the awareness that there is a better way. The first step then in awakening your brother is to get his attention. The presence in you of awareness of the light and your presence in the world of your brother does that.

When your brother begins to awaken and knows that he knoweth not, when the first possibility that specialness is illusory comes to him, he gains the knowledge of the tree of life. This knowledge then sets him surely on the path. Your knowing presence will hasten his journey to the light. And, following the law of giving, will hasten also your journey to the same place.

PART TWO

OF THE ESSENCE

One of Your first statements in reply to what should I be doing was to tell me to write. What does writing do?

> It serves many purposes when you write. It serves your own better understanding and growth and thereby all others. It serves others too who are to read it later.

I see by a review of this journal to this point that I have a pattern of returning to the issue of not getting it and asking why. This is especially true with reference to the relationships that bring the pain, fear, and turmoil.

> Why are you not getting it? Why are you still fearful especially about today and tomorrow?

> A discussion of future and present will need to be gone into when you are further along. For now, let us say that it is symbolic and typical that your struggle is about today and tomorrow as it is about all todays and tomorrows.

> You are getting it in that you have the understanding at an abstract intellectual level. What you do not

have yet is the awareness at other levels that comes through practice; hence, the need for this lesson. Hence the need to see it as a gift and a blessing from a brother who needs you to see it for him as he is not yet ready to see it for himself.

What do I "see" when I look for the Christ in my brother? How do I not see the body? Help me with this.

The body distracts. Just as you were even now distracted from your conscious connection with Me by wandering thoughts from the level of the physical. It is an old and well-established response. It must be consciously broken and replaced with new responses.

Do again now the prescription exercise; Exercise 1.

Then to strengthen your way of seeing, ask, ask, ask. Always and forever ask. Have I not promised that I will help—always and forever? You have come a long way in these months of dealing with this and your impatience is good as long as it is balanced with wisdom.

Now it is time to see the Christ in all. This is the gift of the lesson your brother is bringing.

EXERCISE 2

WHAT YOU SEE IS WHAT YOU GET

Look for the Christ with your new seeing eyes:
The eyes of love
The eyes of knowing
The eyes of compassion
The eyes of truth
The eyes of magic
The eyes of sharing
The eyes of beauty
The eyes of joy
The eyes which only see the things of the Soul
For what you see is what you get.

It is a very common pattern based upon the level of growth of humanity that you hold certain versions of reality that you may or may not be in conscious touch with. You project these out onto the ones whom you see and onto the world that you see. Thus, your own inner concepts become what are reflected back to you. Projection creates perception. What is seen is what is real. Look inside and see only the beauty. Look outside and see projected there only the beauty of your Soul, your Master, the Christ.

Stay in the moment. Know in the moment. There is great joy. Have joy. All will be well. All manner of thing will be well.

I seem to have been able to make some progress in more knowing and connecting. This has brought relief in some ways with the issues of interpersonal difficulties, what You have taught me to see as specialness in me and those with whom I now have relationships.

Your relief is good. To the extent that it is based upon recognition of the Soul, the Christ in your brother, it is sustainable. You are wary though because to return to reliance on the personality to remain steady is no longer acceptable.

Make peace as you can at the level of the personalities while still holding your own center. Do not try to directly move your brother's personality. The power, remember, is in your connectedness. Your awareness and being in that light is what allows you to see beyond the little ego to the part of him that is the very same as that in you. This recognition is what creates the moment of remembering in your brother. With this inner change of focus then comes the outer change. It follows as night follows day.

The little ego would have you be on guard. The remembered connection to Me would have you need no defense. The fear of the next attack is what has you. You see that you have much to lose. This seeing is through the eyes of the ego. It can't see that there is no attack and nothing to lose. As long as you believe you can be attacked, you will see this possibility. What you see is what you get.

When you let go of what you think of as everything, you actually then gain all that is. Your little ego has your world upside down and backward. What you think of as the future will soon be the past; thus, the admonition to have joy. Joy is the natural state in which all needs are met at every moment and you cannot lose the all since nothing else there is.

Child of God! Think of your brother as an infant. It is at this age that you still see the divinity in the child. In the very countenance of the little one is to be beheld the Soul, and the Christ within. Even then if this little one is at the stage of development of a toddler and begins to engage the physical world in ways that may cause you concern for its safety or momentary fear that its actions may harm another, you still see and are reminded by its very presence of the Christ within. Make it thus with your brother. See the Child of God within. Let his appearance be first the reminder of the same Spirit that unites you and then your own call, your own cue, and your prompt to see only the Christ, for that is all there is.

When what you see as attack, betrayal, etc. occurs, it is the ego response that continues to hold you as you respond with hurt and disappointment. This is the little ego engaging its specialness agenda. How could my brother do this to me you say? Learn to recognize in yourself that behavior for it indicates your continuing to allow the belief that your brother can actually disappoint and/or harm you in some way. It is yet another example of sustaining the belief you can actually be hurt by your brother. It is also at the very same time an example of your brother's call for you to remember your wholeness and to bring to him that presence which will make for his own healing.

There is no attack and you do not need to judge.

Yes, we will get onto other matters but this lesson is of the essence and must be mastered.

Following another series of attacks I am able to see the greater perspective but am also aware that I have anger and fear. I seem to be actually holding the energy of an attack. This energy is very painful. How do I move this energy?

First become aware of it. Then cleanse both you and your brother with light.

I know you are weary of this. Let the measure of your weariness be in proportion to your desire to master your little ego.

You have come so far. Return to an indulgent state will only prolong your fear. Indeed it is this state from which the fear comes.

Your mother too is reacting from the lower. It is hard for your little specialness to hear her call for help and not react with the desire to go and help. Additionally, your lower self gets reinforced from such and this is a lesson in true compassion which lies ahead.

Rest. Rest. You are seeing here how your fatigue is blocking the flow. But also know that you have the fatigue because you carry so much armor. You carry the armor because you fear attack and also because you doubt still your own power to heal. It is heavy. Joy is light. Joy will have you levitating with its lightness. See and learn and practice this difference. It will set you free.

Trying to work as instructed here has resulted in my feeling much better.

The energy has moved. Your relief is palpable and now you need to build upon it.

Seeing the divine, the Christ in your brother was instrumental in the healing that you both have experienced. Others now need your healing. Never doubt that your actual thoughts in making this connection were directly the cause of precipitating the moment of the miracle, the moment of healing for you both. Just as others have done for you and just as others now need.

Move now to broaden and deepen your understanding and practice.

How?

Discipline yourself to look first for the Christ in all that you meet. Make it so that it is not an afterthought or add on that comes only when called by pain. Seek to have your mechanism of perception tuned at every moment to be readily, eagerly perceptive of the divinity in all things.

First, proactively shorten the time between your encounter of the brother and the tendency to read the situation in terms of the lower and the point where you wake up and adjust your consciousness to reflect the higher. You are still behind this curve. Practice getting to the level of actively being connected. Do this as an initial reaction (not secondary reaction) seeing your brothers on first contact as the divine beings that they already are. Then as you shorten this time more and more you will be able to establish a new response pattern where your initial position and sustained positioning for perception will be literally at a higher level of consciousness. You will be assisted then to empower, energize and heal those sent to you as a matter of course because you will be focused first on seeing the Christ in them. When this response on your part then becomes automatic, you will become a healer and can be used by your Master and the Masters of Wisdom as a reliable worker. You have been instructed to seek first the Kingdom of God. You have also been told to first be sure you are right and then to go ahead.

This is known as active intelligence and is one of the ways of describing God.

Remember your fundamentals. Get and stay connected to the light. Then your very connectedness does the same for your brother. He then is healed. He is healed by the light and his healing is for all, including you.

You are just to be. Be centered. Be aware of your own divinity. Be consciously aware at every moment of the Christ within you. Look inside and see Him. From this position you will work miracles. You will be the miracle as well as the miracle worker. None will stand against you when they can see that you are One with them.

This is done through the power of love. This is why the Master commanded us to love one another.

Why does this not just happen?

You do reach a point where it does just happen. This is known by many names and is often referred to in its more permanent forms as enlightenment. However, along the way, the path, one must overcome the little ego. It is the little ego that first creates the fear that you have actually separated yourself from God—an absurd notion. The little ego then sets about to protect you from the fear of the truth and wraps you in a casement designed to make you think you are protected from that fear but that is in reality an insulator so as to keep you from seeing the truth that is the fundamental falseness of the little ego. This is your armor of doubt.

Part of your armor of doubt is enabled by your thoughts of your own littleness. Believing that you are not somehow worthy or deserving of the light, attention of the Master, gift of the Holy Spirit, peace of God or even love of God creates a fundamental inability to receive. To receive you must believe. If you see yourself as not worthy then by definition you are not worthy.

Getting above your thoughts of your own littleness allows what is your more natural state, constant contact with Me, to flow. Reverting to that thought stops the flow and returns you to dependence on the little ego. The little ego who uses fear to control you and who has a vested interest in remaining in control and not in the flow also has then a madness to its method in that encouraging your sense of unworthiness feeds your doubt which blocks your acceptance of awareness of and connection to Me.

I have heard of my armor of doubt before from a brother who gave me a number of insights into my seeking to learn more of things Spiritual. Tell me more of this please.

At its most essential, the armor of doubt is predicated upon a foolish presumption of unworthiness. This alone is a true madness which is like in its functional expression unto to that of your movie *The Matrix,* in which there is a reality below the level of waking understanding which is maintained so well that it isn't even seen. It is analogous to the ancient concept that the fish will be the last to recognize the water.

That foolish presumption that then masks all other truth is that you could actually be of little to no value to the One Who created you. While the truth is that you are a created son of the One Father made in His very exact image. The truth is that God is love and you are 100 percent of the same fabric, kin, and essence of Him that loved you so as to create you.

So, instead of unworthiness, like everything that the ego has had you buy, the opposite is actually true. You are of profound worth in this and any Universe. My God! You are the son of God! As such, your worth is beyond any statement of value. There is not and literally cannot be such a statement but there is a number that can be placed upon it. It is the single largest number in the Universe of which any other numerical expression, no matter how large, is but a fraction.

It is the primal, ordinal, quintessential, and irreducible number, One. You carry the value of, are of, and are One with the Father. What is your value then? One, the greatest of all enumerations!

By the way, interesting bit of histrionics there.

You are welcome. It was for your benefit as well as some who will eventually read this and need a bit of histrionics to get their attention to this vital point.

Even with the histrionics, obviously I am not getting this yet. It is an inspiring thought but . . .

It is the "but" here that shows your armor of doubt.

This is indeed a grand, sweeping and breathtaking concept. It is of such a truth, and so breathtaking that at the end of what you consider life, meaning the death of the body, you do literally have what you now think of as your breath taken, so that you may join the next steps toward integrating your understanding of the joy of this Oneness. When seen then from the side of the higher, the Soul, your breath is not in the last moments taken away. You give it gladly for you begin to glimpse the Truth and grow impatient to move into it. The grand, beyond your ability to understand as yet, most fundamental, undividable and foundational of all Truth: You are nothing less than a son of the One Father and are One in Him with all that Is, including all, every one, of your brothers and sisters.

Holy stuff!

What you really want to say is "Holy Shit."

True.

Then do that.

Holy Shit!

Amen!

PART THREE

OF FAITH AND FLIGHT

I have been told to let my faith take me higher.

One of the primary concepts and bits of memory that is carried so deep in yourselves as to not be completely masked or completely fooled by the ego's falseness is faith itself. Faith is not just a perception; it is an understanding that has been hardwired into all of Creation. It is an actual function, a tool, a way of shedding your armor of doubt. Faith is the still small voice or the thunderous sudden awareness that there is a greater thing of which you are a great, grand, and undivided part.

Faith is what is built upon as well as built via the process of asserting your connectedness to your brother and to all things. This process gives you first, working example and then concrete experience that it exists and can happen. Then you begin to see that you may affect it by calling it to happen. Next you begin to realize that you can actually create it at will. Then you come to see that you are not so much creating it as tapping at will what is already there. This is followed by the understanding that you can sustain this connectedness. This last state of consciousness prepares the way to return to the beginning and realize that you are the flow itself and that this is your natural state into which you must only rest. You then have achieved the re-membering. You have remembered for this is the state in which you, with all your brothers, exist in the mind of God. This is the state into which you were first conceived even before the world was made. This is the true state, the one constant and the only reality. All else is illusion. All else is a forgetting.

You are this state of Being. In it We, you, your brother and I are One. This is life.

Come to life to Me—through Me.

How is this dialogue, this conversation, actually working? What is the mechanism or the trigger for us to talk?

The messages come, are initiated and actually triggered as you physically sit and put your vehicles together in the effort.

This includes the act of placing your hand with the pen to the paper or hands to the keyboard. These synchronize you to receive.

Lord this is a wonderful thing! Thank You!

Will not the time come when I will have the sense of being connected to You moment by moment? That is, all the time and not needing the focus of the writing?

You have already experienced moments of knowing that were not connected to your actual writing. The answer is yes. The OM helps as you were told by your brother and teacher of a few years ago. Sound it inwardly as you have done thousands of times now. You are learning to overcome the distraction of the lower. Practice is what you need.

Also, to refer to Me as Lord is not on the mark. It would be closer to refer to Me, if you must objectify Me, as we or us, for that is how close we actually are. Knowing that this is difficult in words should not keep you from working on the greater understanding of this bedrock concept.

There are true Masters, the Masters of Wisdom, for whom the title Lord is lovingly appropriate; more on Them later.

I had a dream many months ago that I was very high up in the sky and saw the Earth in a different way. It was higher than any flight in a plane. I also had an impression that there was more to come. My first thoughts were that this kind of dream is not uncommon to me as I have loved both the idea and the fact of flight all my life.

Your dream of last year of being high in the sky was indeed a foretaste of some moments to come. Thoughts of flight including the wish to engage in physical flight are latent in faith. Everyone has these thoughts in some form. The concept is seed-like in your faith and as it blossoms helps you to recognize your faith and become more in touch with this very powerful tool of awakening. Thus it is that dreams both in the waking state and the sleeping dream state of most of you, your brothers, will at times contain images of flying and views of the Earth from above. This can be read as simple metaphor or seen as potent images of the hidden truth of who you really are and your desire, your need, to be reconnected, to re-member that which you are. Thus, you often use and hear the term, flight of faith.

It is this new ability to understand that you have faith and to grasp it as real, that is, to actually see it, that our first exercise was given so as to install a new clarity of vision.

Since that dream, levitation or even actual flight has once again come into my thoughts as a possibility as they once were in my childhood. You have told me that the joy would cause or allow this. I took that to mean figuratively. Could it be that it may also be a physical happening as well?

First have joy. As you have been instructed, first seek the Kingdom of God . . . Yes this can be. You would have to want it for the right reasons and it would have to be right in terms of the time. It would also be a byproduct and not an end. The little ego would want it as an end for self-aggrandizement.

I understand that wanting to serve the Plan would be the right reason.

This would be true.

Why am I not amazed with this seemingly new opening in my life to a loving wisdom that I may actually converse with?

You once were. As noted earlier, you are more used to hearing Me now. The original thrill has been replaced with an acceptance and growing understanding that allows you to move past the rush into more and more sustaining of the communion. Me, you may take for granted. As I told you, I am here always and you may rely absolutely on that. All you must do to reopen the door is to ask and then listen. You are still at the point where you do not listen all the time. When you get to where you listen all the time you will see the connection all the time. It is now up to you to grow into the constant connecting using your creative imagination and other higher level functions so as to keep your point of connection to Me at a conscious level.

You have had an image of your physical body being surrounded by a glow that follows the outline of your torso. This is Me. So, when I tell you that there is not a time when we are not connected, it is more true than you yet sense because we are more than connected. We are One. We are the One in whom you live and move and have our being. Just as I in turn am so connected to a greater One. But as we, you and I, are One, so are we, you and I and Him, One. There is not separation of any kind. There is no seam. There is not a moment when the continuity of the Oneness is not. There is only your waking up to it and your being able to stay attuned. Your starts and stops represent gaps in your perception only, not in the reality of the Oneness. And, I miss you when you are gone from the consciousness of the connection.

This seems so normal as to be unspectacular, almost.

It is the natural state and you should be comfortable in it. The promised bliss lies ahead as you are still working on your instrument and improving your command of your vehicles. As this unfolds you will be able to attune more and more to the totality of the content. This will mean getting more regularly into the flow and more aware of the connection. In time it will be the most natural thing in the world, remarkable only when it is not in your awareness. When you reach the point that you miss Me when you are gone from the consciousness of the connection, you will have achieved awareness of the flow as a part of your make up and not just something that we do in the small hours of the morning or when you experience sufficient pain so as to cry for help. This will come.

Enough for now, you are fatigued. Continue with the activity aimed at returning more vitality to your physical body. This will help with the connection. It, too, is one of your vehicles.

Okay. Next time may we connect some on the greater One?

If you wish.

Thank You.

PART FOUR

THE GREATER ONE

Our connectedness is now such you may go directly to the machine or paper without doing your customary start-up centering.

The One in whom We live and move and have our being is the greater One. We are a creation of and exist in the mind of this One. God is what most name Him though with reference to gender, "It" is closer to accurate. To say, however, that We exist here is to imply a passiveness that is not so. We are Creation in the same way that I have encouraged you to be the flow. We are endowed by the Creator in direct proportion to our ability to absorb, reflect and be Him. Remember that We are in His image. The endowments include most definitely the power to create. It is again a proactive capacity that carries not just a potential but an assumed functioning. It is not just that We are gifted with the potential, but We are so created that We cannot not create. It is up to us to learn how to wield this power or energy in such a way as to serve the Plan of the Creator. When We are doing so, We are in the flow and in so being are functioning as not just an extension of the Creator but are literally of the Creator and in the process of Creation. We become One with Him. We become Him. We become One with and are Being Itself. And It becomes Us.

Thus, while all of the metaphors you have heard such as "I am closer than your hand and your very thoughts" are true as far as they go; they do not go far enough, for the reverse is also true. You are closer to Me than your hand. So close in fact that the concept of close does not apply. Concepts such as unified, indistinguishable, melded, homogenized, and integrated are closer to the mark. However, to the extent that these still imply any separation whatsoever, they too are short of the reality. The reality simply is that we are not distinguishable one from the other because we are the very same. We are One.

This does not mean that you are not able to rightly see yourself as a distinct and recognizable subunit of the Us that can conceive of Itself as such. This is also part of the reality. However, the perceptual error occurs when you know yourself to be unique within Creation and mistakenly see that grand uniqueness as separateness. This is not so and is as if parts of your physical body were to achieve independence of thought and use that great gift in error by disintegrating the body. It would be as if your heart were to believe and act as if it were alone and not a functional part of the whole of your body and could start and stop at will ignoring its relationship and mutual dependency on the other organs, parts and systems.

Given therefore, as part of the Creation, as part of the grand design, is this Unity of all things.

So fundamental, foundational, imperative, critical, and quintessentially important is this concept that when asked by the scribe "Which is the first commandment of all?" He who was asked replied "The Lord our God is one Lord".[2] The operative word there being "One." He returned to this simple but requisite concept over and over again as when He said ". . . Every kingdom divided against itself is brought to desolation; and a house divided against a house falleth".[3] He was speaking at many levels and foreshadowed this day where everywhere you look the houses of man are divided and falling.

A way to measure your growth then is in terms of your progress toward recognizing this One reality and realizing your connectedness to it. The path to recognizing that connectedness is through use of the gift of the creative imagination. You literally image yourself as part of the greater reality and in so doing your awareness of that reality is affected, made. You tap the field of energy that is already existing knowledge and in so doing re-member into and with it. This is what you do when you consciously connect to Me. This represents a profoundly creative act.

You just learned, had a concrete example of, how to handle problems, as you were just now confused about how this software works and had a couple of moments of panic thinking that you might lose this morning's work. You then tried a few best guesses and when they did not work paused to allow the panic to subside and then you asked for help. The help then came. Did it not? You also got the idea to go to auto backup as the better long-term solution in this case.

In time the interval between recognizing your unconnectedness and acting to re-member will grow shorter until the time away will be the exception and then only because you have no immediate need of the awareness because you will be working at a higher level.

This higher level will be one where you are more autonomous as needed because you will have learned what the One would have you do and it will not be necessary to consult for direction as often. However, there will never, ever be a time when you will not be able to call on Me directly. *This level of functioning will be more characterized by a quiet knowing that we are connected all the time and the comfort of that knowledge will let you move more freely and more widely in the world.* It is the state of individuation based on the knowledge of unity and is never separating but is only empowering. At this level you can be relied upon to be a worker and can be called upon by the Masters of Wisdom, Whose work it is to implement the Plan.

This work is of you, also. True, I have, as you say, all the answers, but that is not to say that you have no say. Your love/wisdom is more than an inextricable link here. Thus is the nature of Creation; your cooperation calls for your ownership and empowers you to become an active and involved partner in the process, its direction, and outcomes.

We will embark on the book as soon as you are ready. You will know and I will know when that is. It is near. For the short run your continued practice is required. The training of your vehicles to refocus on Me and our connectedness is in need of furthering. Fortunately, opportunities for practice are abundant. One was your generally successful reception of the intrusive moment of a few minutes ago when your attention on the material plane was requested and you decided to give that attention and then to return to this narrative

Any further suggestions on ways to get to and hold the connection, ways to more readily see, stay in, and be the light?

Your question implies much growth. This is good. In addition to the answers, which you know, I will make a couple of suggestions of "tricks of the trade" as you say.

Have a routine of coming to focal points in your day. These can be benchmarks of a sort so that you arrive there and check your status. Noontime meditation would be such a focal point.

It would also help if you had physical points of reminder. These could be objects charged by you with meaning so that they become indicators to you to confirm your awareness and refocus as needed. Your screensaver has been such a point. Continue that practice and remember, there is no inappropriate activity relative to your being in the flow and moment to moment consciously aware of the connection, none. Everything that you first think, and then do will take on a different level of capacity and wonder when you get the filters of the lower mind and little ego out of the way and just be. You have been told by the Master "What you think of as the future will soon be the past."

Other points in the physical environment will work well. Remember too, you have help here because the natural world, when seen through the eyes of those aspiring to see, is itself a call to re-member. Indeed that is what it is there for. Rocks, trees, birds, clouds, grass, dirt, water, air and the very gravity which holds you, are all pieces of the greater whole and each can serve to, in an instant, re-mind you of and give you capture of the underlying Unity of all things.

Opportunities for discovery of joy lay literally with each step. It is a construct in the program of life itself. The whole is each part and calls constantly to each part, and thus keeps re-minding you until you are awakened. There exists a veritable symphony that you walk through all the time. It is there to call you to the beauty and to be thus re-minded of the connection that you bear and are to all things. The Universe is a hologram. The smallest particle contains the whole and can be used for instant reconnection to that whole.

Gravity is an expression of the love nature of God. As a mother holds her child so God holds you here in your infancy. You can and will grow to the point where release will be the appropriate and equally loving response. Transition to this point is now foreseeable. Even though it is equally true that space exploration has become one of the more overtly shared and cooperative experience-based activities, especially during the last several years, your progress here is retarded by the sense of separation.

A major vehicle for the expression of separation is competition. Your first steps into space are a good model of how evolution toward cooperation and sharing is unfolding. Early steps were characterized by military response to fear. Now those who were once enemies and rivals are working together on the space station. The participation by other nations is also an indicator of this evolution toward sharing and cooperation.

I am beginning to sense a larger field here than the answers to my own questions. How may this work, this dialogue be used, if at all, other than as the wonderful opening I asked for?

This material is first for you then, later, for others. It is to help you grow Spiritually as that is what you have been asking for.

My understanding is that to grow Spiritually one can profit from study, meditation, and service. I have been working on all three for some time with what I would say is some success and mostly not.

We will need to return many times to the implied self-criticism and doubt in that question. For now let it be said that the time has come to grow beyond those limiting concepts. The larger field you sense is indeed part of the greater setting of this work and involves all three of the arenas of Spiritual practice for growth as you now understand them. The world of your study, as you have been much about study now for many years, will be significant to this work and the journal that will be among its results.

Okay. In my study I have returned over and over again to the teachings by and about the Masters of Wisdom and also to <u>A Course In Miracles</u>. Both are very full, dense, and seemingly complete. How is it that I, this work, could add even one jot to those great pieces of work?

> As you suggest, adding would not be needed. You are to help bridge and render one into the context of the other and not just these teachings but many traditions of which you have become familiar including the King James Version and other works representing the great religions of the world as well as the great philosophies of the world. You are not to represent yourself as expert but as one who is sufficiently grounded so as to further the awareness of and understanding of the unity of all knowledge and the Plan.
>
> The awakening of your brother is your true life's work. What has gone before was mere distraction.
>
> Your work is first and foremost a privilege to assist your brother in his awakening. Secondly, it is your sacred obligation as it serves God's Plan of evolution. Third, it is your own salvation.
>
> By doing the work of awakening you get worked on. You are further schooled, informed, exposed, and enlightened so that you are more capable. This growth on your part progressively equips you to better serve and in the serving you learn how to better yet serve. It is an infinite progression with each turn of the spiral informing and enhancing the next. It is Alpha and Omega. Thus, working for your brother's salvation ensures your own.

All serve the Plan in that all things work together for the greater good. This is a given. Even those who say they do not serve the Plan do serve the Plan. They are just not yet at the point of doing so with awareness, understanding, and efficiency. Also, many serve at high levels of contribution without the knowledge of the greater context of the Hierarchy of the Masters of Wisdom, works such as <u>A Course In Miracles</u> or the Plan itself. They are hearing their Soul and acting.

Each person has a unique part of the Plan that they may assist into manifestation. The uniqueness of each is evidence of their so being equipped. Mastering your ability to discern your part of the Plan and then acting to do the service is the call of each person.

The Plan is the thought of the Creator revealed to us. It is nothing less than His word being manifest and rendered tangible; that is, material. It is inherently sacred and as it is of the One in Whom we live and move and have our being, we have a sacred obligation to serve this Plan. Indeed we will serve this Plan. We cannot not serve the Plan. To do so with understanding is to have joy. To do so from the perspective of not having this understanding or with the fear-based resistance of the unawakened little self is to be dragged, kicking and screaming, to the gates of heaven. It is ultimately the choice of each as to when to wake up. But there is no choice whether to awaken or not for the awakening is in the Plan.

This awakening then is a privilege, for God needs us up and running. The Plan is not simply to awaken all, though this is the immediate work, it is so that the awakened all can then serve ever greater levels of the Plan and bring to manifestation the very will of the Creator through becoming fully cognizant and volitional parts themselves; partners in the process, partners in the advancement, partners in the unfolding and ultimately, partners in Creation itself.

God has never stopped creating. It is an ongoing process. The more who are awakened to become actively aware and co-creating with God, the more of the Plan that can be implemented. Implementation then allows for more evolution. This is the true meaning of the book of life and it has no final chapter. It is infinite.

If "The awakening of your brother is your true life's work", how do I go about this?

This world has the gift of arriving at harmony through conflict. It is the most basic of all learning paradigms on Earth. Indeed it is the great discomfort of such that has contributed to your issuing the call for God's 800 number. So let us start there.

When your brother displays anger, jealousy, judgment, attack of any kind, or anything of the lower, let that be a sign unto you. Read this sign as the call for love that it is. Retrain your vehicles to perceive this behavior in the light of higher truth and let it trigger the proper response of the Soul and not the currently typical response of the lower, that is, of the personality, of the little ego.

Respond to it as you would to the distress cry of a baby—that sound that everyone knows so well and is so compelling that it may not be ignored. It reaches to the depths of your being and demands, requires, that you respond. Most choose to respond to the cry of a baby with concern, compassion, and care. Make this then the response when your brother calls. Reject not him because he cries. It is the same cry as that of the baby. The only difference is that it is from a chronologically older body. But it comes just the same from a babe, a heavenly babe who is your brother and literally crying out for your help.

In the upside down world that your little ego has created, this cry is seen as attack or a cause to judge your brother and find him wanting in some way so as to permit the conclusion that you are separate from him. The conclusion of separateness is the illusion and it requires constant maintenance. So the little ego has its measuring stick out all the time seeking comparison upon which it may perseverate in judging. This it invariably finds because it looks for it all the time. It is a self-fulfilling prophecy because what you see is what you get.

Nothing can withstand this level of scrutiny and judgment for this is a mechanism designed to allow nothing to withstand it. The little self has constructed a self-priming, self-starting, self-stopping, self-perpetuating circle of measurement and judgment which is unerring in its capacity to deliver and reinforce the message that you are separate from your brother.

This perception of separation takes two forms and it matters not which form for they both lead to the same conclusion. Either you decide that your brother is inferior to you in some way because, after all, you would never do whatever it is you are judging that he has done or is doing. Or you conclude that he is displaying behavior or physical characteristics, or material things which you do not possess or are not capable of generating. In this case you judge him to be superior to you. Your little ego chooses to see then that you are either superior or inferior. Either choice brings with it the continuation of the conclusion and maintenance of the illusion that you are separate. Once you have confirmed again your lack of connection and your separation, you feel justified in either attacking him or denying him what he needs to be whole and holy.

This then is the trap of the lower that you are called upon to see and avoid. The miracle is that when you see and avoid this trap, you set up the condition for your brother to awaken and break out of the circle of self-fulfilling prophecy of the little ego and its vehicle—the personality. Your very act of reconnecting is for both of you and produces results for the both of you.

So when you see your brother engaging in judgment and concluding that he is either superior or inferior to his brothers, see that as error. It is your signal to know that he has judged himself as separate. This requires healing. You are privileged to help him heal by positioning yourself to see for him what he has temporarily lost sight of, the Christ in all. By responding for him, you call him to look

again and again until he too can see with the
eyes of love and not through the eyes of fear or
one of the manifestations of fear, the illusion of
superiority or inferiority. By responding for him,
you help him heal and shorten to a holy instant
the time to his awakening.

Or, you yourself may choose to accept your
brother's judgment and buy into the illusion in
which case you confirm and perpetuate the self-
fulfilling prophecy of his little ego and your own.
This is the seduction of the lower and easy to do
until you remember and see it for what it is. This
is the tacit conspiracy of all little egos that will
judge and choose to see each other as separate
but will unite in denying even the possibility of
the greater whole. The threat to the little ego is so
great because it is in proportion to its capacity to
bring the light of the Soul, and thus healing, to
the level of the ego where the light is feared and
not wanted. Thus, even though it is a kingdom of
one, the little ego will unite with other little ones
and literally fight to remain in the darkness of its
self-imposed littleness and separation. It will run
from the safety of the light into the darkness of
the fear. Hence you will see all manner of behavior
aimed at thwarting the light. This will include ego
attack aimed at anything that would bring light,
including you.

The denial and subsequent coping behavior in
maintaining the illusion of the separation of the
little ego is well developed and automatic to it. It
is so well developed that for many the thought
that there is a better way is not even possible. He
knoweth not that he knoweth not. It is from this

state that your brother will attack. His attack then is a cry for help. He needs and the Plan requires your help for him so that he may move from this state; yet so strong is the illusion, he will resist and attack again. Thus, you must deal with it, in fact can only deal with it, from the higher level of first re-membering for the both of you and holding your connectedness up to and for him. This is an act of love, which requires that you give up, that you sacrifice your own illusion of separateness. You must give up the very life of your own little ego first. Then and only then may you help him. Thus, it is truly said that greater love hath no man but that he give up his own life.

There is a term that I have encountered many times in my studies and that is hard to learn. It is that of connection. You seem to be touching on it here. To respond to my brother's call for help and love, it would seem that I must somehow connect with him.

The connectedness has a greater dimension than that discussed so far. It reflects a higher truth and a higher function also. Analogous to the brain of a newborn that has nerve cells in place but must grow into its intellectual capacity via connecting them is the connectedness that I am calling upon you and all your brothers to grow into. Humankind has a function as a whole. You will serve not only at the individual level but also at the group level. Indeed the new age is the age of the group.

In order to grow your capacity for ever greater knowledge and the ability to express it through ever greater creativity and service, you must connect to and become One with each other just as the brain cells of the infant must so connect. Resulting from the connectedness will be a new entity. Truly united in this way, mankind will be able to consciously act at a whole new level, a holy new level, just as the brain of the infant gains capacity until it too functions as a whole with corresponding geometric leaps in capacity.

Thus, is the pattern of Creation. Ever does the lesser part unite with its brothers to form, to become, the next greater part, which in turn unites with its brothers, etc. From the connection of the individual brain cells to their connection to the greater thing we call mind to the connection of galaxies to form the greater thing we call Universe, the pattern holds true. It is truly said therefore, "As above so below."

This morning's work seems to have come harder than usual. There have been several periods of total loss of focus. How much of the malaise of the last 90 minutes has been from what cause?

Child of God—you are so very close. Be of good cheer and confidence. All will be well.

Fatigue was at work this morning. You could sense the higher concepts but could not get to them. Go back to that theme again when you are more rested.

Can You recommend a schedule that would be better than the 3:30 a.m. schedule we are now on?

No. You manage the physical body. You will know what works. Rest more, yes. But also know that much of the fatigue is from the unnecessary weight you carry in the form of stress caused by the constant judging by the little ego. This, added to the remnants of your doubt, though improved, remains heavy. Joy is light. Have only joy (you have recently had such a time) and watch your burden evaporate and your weariness go.

When I am really centered, that is connected, I do have a sense of a different intellect and voice in Your words than what I would normally associate with my own thought patterns, language, and the general workings of the voice in my head. However, I also do not have a sense of the words being really different from me. It is as if they are Your words but are just as much mine also and at the same time.

They are your words just as much as they are Mine. When you are at the level of connection you are the words.

You said ". . . you are so very close". That is reassuring and I am grateful. I will take all the help I can get. Close to what?

To greater awareness of union with Me and all that is. To a new level of that knowledge which will bring the peace that passeth understanding. To the peace of God that is after all the only thing you really want and the only thing worth having and in reality, the only thing. Close to the breakthrough that will deliver you finally from the doubt. As I told you, there has been progress here. Indeed on all fronts.

I hear you when you say that you want to move on from where you are. Now you hear Me. Your joy will fill the earth and give you the gift of empowering others to that joy. You will be a bearer of light to those in darkness. You will need only the awareness of their need to trigger your loving response, which will be a joy to you. Truly meeting your brother's need will be true joy for you. It will be child's play. You will laugh, dance, sing, and play. It is close to the playground that you are. The battleground is fading.

As I read much of the last several entries I see a restating of some of the beautiful principles of <u>A Course In Miracles</u>. Anyone could read this for themselves?

Do not be concerned about duplicating any of the great pieces of which you have become aware. That is not what we are about. You properly see that they stand on their own themes and merit. It is the bridging, the connecting of one body of wisdom to that of another, that we are about. You imply that all anyone must do is to read what you have read and they can see it for themselves, that you do not see that your work here would be significant. It will be a map for those who need help in locating their place relative to the materials that you have found. Remember that you too had, and continue to have, such help. Remember also how long you have taken to get here. Your work will be about shortening the time. It will be about putting bridges and signposts in place for your brother so that he will benefit from your path's knowledge and not have to wander as much as you. It will be about your sharing. It will be about your shedding light onto his path. It will be about beckoning to him to come out of his fear and to take your hand in his to walk the higher path with you. It will be about your own moving to higher ground which can only come about as you assist him, your brother. Thus is the gift of the power to empower. Such is the thirst of the flock of which you are a member. You are all thirsty for such is what has awakened in your heart and will burst forth to be shared. Indeed you may not contain it. You may deny it no longer.

You were given examples but only a few days ago when, in a conversation upon Spiritual growth, it was said to you that many are come to the point of suddenly making the turn to knowing that they are ready and they are asking for help and guidance, as you once did not too long ago. You then were given the specific example of a sister responding to your guidance about her own fear and who was ready and quick to take the empowerment you were privileged to share with her. Others there are. See them as little babes just waking up. They are all around you. They are stirring. They need love, wisdom and direction. They are calling out to the world for it and God has sent you to them. And God has sent them to you. They bless you with their presence as you bless them with yours. It is the perfect match. It is an example of why it is truly said that this is a perfect world.

Your work then, the book and what will come of it, has already begun. Yes, you will be offered the opportunity to help in the work done by others. It will not be as you might see it from your current perspective. What you think of as the future will soon be the past.

The immediate circle will widen and ripple. Look for its unfolding. Look to your brother for the moment of his readiness to make the turn, to be open, and you be ready to grasp that moment for the both of you. It will come and you will get better at reading signs of its happening. You will be able to sense it and anticipate it so as to ready yourself as needed.

Know all this to be true. Know this to be your calling. Know that you are ready and you will be ready. Know this joy and it will set you free.

It is this then that you are so close to. It is this then that is the temple that you must enter. Expect it. It will literally take your breath away and your breath will be replaced with the breath of the Divine.

It is no longer as you were once told, ". . . far in the distance yet so near." It is now near. You must only knock and keep knocking. Use a progressively heavier hand. Remember you are knocking for many in addition to yourself. This gives your hand weight it has not had before. It conveys responsibility, true, and with that responsibility comes privilege to serve and to act for those whom you serve, those you lead. It gives you privilege to ask in their name and for their need.

Let the measure of their desperation tell you of your capacity to respond. These are in direct proportion one to the other. They are in such pain that they will strike out at anyone, even you. Thus, your loathsome attackers are truly but your brothers and sisters seeking direction. Turn the energy of the attack around and transform it into the energy of their liberation. Of this you already have many concrete examples, not only the specific one in your mind of this moment which you now recall correctly. Use them as examples and learn from them.

I am given to understand that when used, the words *"you" and "your"*, *except where clearly delineated otherwise, are meant to be in the plural.*

You got that right!

Go rest and be blessed.

PART FIVE

BE IN THE WORLD
BUT NOT OF IT

Sitting here now sensing that I am doing so in You. Thank You. And musing, pondering, where we go from here and how we get there.

> There is no "where" to go. When you are connected you are there. You are at/in the state of Being. While it may appear to you that the geography and time may change, these are illusion. To be in the moment and in the awareness is to be in the natural state.
>
> Your impatience with places, both geographic and of activity and mental states, which detract from the connectedness, that indeed are designed by the little ego to do just that, is growing. Take that as a signpost. You are less and less able to tolerate these places and loathe the expenditure of energy necessary to push through them. This is part of your fatigue.
>
> This is a lesson in detachment. When you sense that the place is a hindrance to your moving forward,

it is because you are buying into the illusion that it is real. You must be in the world to do the work of serving your brother's awakening. However, you must not be of the world. To be of the world is to remain unawakened. To be detached is to not be of the world. To be detached is to see the battleground from above, in which case it becomes for you the playground. From there, the empowering of your brother to also achieve this perspective becomes but child's play.

This then is where you are going, this place out of time and space (at least as you have conceptualized them until now). This is the state discovered by your imagination and secured by your faith. This is the place of awareness, the place of connectedness, the place of knowing, the place of joy, the place where all becomes play, the place of remembering, and the place of sweet reunion. This then is heaven.

You get there through being there, being with Me. Watch Me and I will show you Being. You will be able to see Me Being. Be there.

Faith, too, is something that you must only remember. It is naturally there in the child and is reinforced on the physical level by virtue of the child's being dependent upon others for all its needs. The child that is welcomed into the world with love and support knows that it is taken care of. The child knows that there is always home and that is where it only must go to be safe and reassured. This understanding is empowering. It allows the child the framework within which to naturally and spontaneously give. It is the simple extension of this childlike understanding that causes the act of giving. This grounds the faith in the physical level by giving. This too is a natural act for it is born out of the understanding that everyone has a home and that all can go there and be safe and understood.

The natural spontaneous giving which comes from this understanding has the effect of creating and rendering manifest on the physical plane, faith. This is so because giving within the context of this understanding assures receiving. Giving not only completes the cycle, it also energizes the circle and guarantees that receiving occurs because completing and energizing the circle starts the cycle again. To receive only and not give is to stop the cycle and both dam and damn the flow.

It is the giving then and not the receiving that is the creative act. It is the giving that is the re-membering. Thus, it is truly said that it is more blessed to give than to receive.

It was just such a gift that started the cycle and permitted loaves and fishes to be multiplied to feed all that were on the mount that day.

First that day was the gift, given in childlike understanding of the abundance inherent in the Plan and it thus energized the cycle. This provided the energy, the love, for Jesus, who understood the connectedness, to multiply the gift a thousand fold. When within the childlike connectedness, when in the natural state and not separated, this all brothers can do and spontaneously do.

DIALOGUES WITH THE HOLY SPIRIT

I have been told that all I must do is to ask for the help I need. I am asking. Help me see the Christ always in everyone. Help me move to the place that is so close. Help me "see" whatever I need to see in my brother so as to render me connected. Help me heal myself with my own vision and so heal us all. Help me see the moment of my brother's readiness as You indicated I would. It all sounds like what I have asked for and what I will take joy in doing. Help me move to detachment. This I ask and more. Help me by giving me what I need to make these moves. And most of all help me with the fear, the fear that paralyzes me and renders me unconnected. Help me to unerringly focus on that point of joy where remembering is the natural state and to use the gift of denial to not give credence to any of the lower.

> Very well, no tall order really. I will help you as I have done so for a long time. Remember that I told you that I miss you when you are away from the connectedness with your brother and Me. I have been calling to you for a long time. Sometimes I could get your attention and sometimes I could not.

> The concerns about work and some of the relationships there continue to be exaggerated. This is part of your fear. A sea change has occurred and will slowly become manifest. You are there to assist its unfolding. Bring the joy and share it with all there. Much good has already been done. Let your natural state flow to others. They will receive it well. Know you are ready and you will be ready.

How will You be helping? What do I look or listen for specifically?

Signs, signals, and callings have been placed already in the environment. They abound. They are part of what you must point out as the help to your brother. You rightly deduce that you first must see them.

Look for things that bring a smile instantly. Look for the juxtaposition of symbols. These are not accidents. You have so often told others that there are no accidents. This is true. Know it yourself.

A good example is the regret and remorse you felt when one of your beloved trees had to be removed because it was dying and had become a danger to others. The day after it had been removed you were walking past and saw the full moon directly over the spot where it had been. This stopped you in your tracks as it was designed to do and you were able to draw the proper conclusion of the Unity of all things and the passing of that which has fulfilled its purpose and being and whose time has come.

It is like the new meditation given by the Masters of Wisdom called Transmission Meditation. This you have learned and in so doing have been taught that you must constantly be returning to the point of focus. After doing it over and over again you get a little better and a little better until it becomes automatic just as breathing is automatic. You are at the doing it over and over again stage. Get on with it.

The way to automatic is through practice and sharing. The practice is discipline you must cultivate. The sharing does several things. It reinforces the practice in you. It also multiplies those in the field who are moving to knowing that they too are ready to make the turn and gives them a point to turn to. In this way you become both the compass and the content for their cry for direction. As those waking up grow in number, this adds to the ability of all to wake up in less time.

A sister who has been of such help to me keeps coming to mind here. Is there communication for her from You that I could be vehicle for.

Tell her that she is still trying too hard. Tell her that she too is close and could benefit from going with the flow. She needs to know that things at home will work out well and will return to a more soft way. A daily journal will now work better for her and is a good idea.

Another sister is making efforts to grow through and past ego issues. Is there something that You would have me convey to her?

She can see her own growing wisdom as reflected in yours. Tell her that she is loved and protected and that fear is a block to her perception of this.

What can I tell her to help her with her pain and fear?

You already have. From one of your favorite sources tell her "You are a child of the universe, no less than the trees and the stars; you have a right to be here".[4] A healing session will help her. Her awakening to the need to meditate more will give her comfort.

I struggle with the practice. I struggle to handle the fear. I struggle to seek the joy. There are many times when I recognize that the fear is where I am and still cannot seem to move it even though I recognize it. Is some of this related to my physical condition? Is some of this because of the detox stuff I am using? Even as I ask I hear that I should use the technique of visualizing the bringing down of the cleansing white light and the healing golden light.

> Yes to all of the above. You will ask for help at these times. Does this not show you the progress I have told you has come? It is still hard for you to listen when blocked by the fear. You have asked at these times for a talisman or touchstone. The capacity is there. You have seen it. The stone is there; you have reached out for it before. Now you must simply practice. You are given the opportunity to practice then every day because you have asked for help. When the practice comes though it still registers as fear. Know it then as the imposter it is for the fear is the defense of the lower that believes it has something to lose. It sees your opportunity in this light. The truth is that the opportunity is the doorway to the next higher plateau of consciousness, the making and sustaining of the connectedness with Me. "You touch the stone and it turns to light".

What is the stone?

> It is the touchstone of your consciousness. It is the higher self. It is the Christ within you recognizing the Christ in all. It is there for you all the time and all you must do is to reach out to it.

At those times when I at least recognize the fear, I am reaching out. Or, at least I think I am. So what else can I do?

> Stay the course. Know it is there for you and all your brothers. Knock. Continue. Let your frustration motivate you and not stop you. Remember the Buddha's struggle of years. Demand your heavenly birthright. Assault the things that are standing in the way. Storm the gates of heaven.

My anger then which I often express at the little ego is okay?

> To the extent that it allows you to say no; to the extent that it allows you to say that there must be a better way; to the extent that it empowers you to move onto that way, your anger can be a useful tool for now. Do not let it keep you focused on the excesses of the little ego lest you fixate there or even indulge some kind of thoughts of recrimination. To do this would be to fall into the trap of the little ego and buy into its agenda of, in your case, littleness.

I suppose I am asking for a magic bullet that will allow me to just get on with it.

> Your faith is such a thing. It needs strengthening. This you must do. This you must create. This you must earn so that it will be yours. Your creating of it will give you ownership and full function in that awareness. Otherwise you would always be encountering circumstances where the next test would have you asking for another bullet instead of knowing you already have all that you need.

There is an easy way out. There is the way of all that have successfully traveled this path before you. Let go of the things of the lower. Others have done this. So can you. So will you.

Eat more often and eat more variety. You may do this now. Return to some physical exercise.

Most of all have the joy that you know is already there. Have it for you have been given it by the Father. You have not earned it; it was gifted to you in the original Creation, as the Father wanted all of Creation to have His attributes of love and joy. What you have earned is the knowledge that it is your birthright. This then is your ultimate touchstone. "You touch the stone and it turns to light". Do this and liberate yourself and your brother.

Did I hear correctly that I should not write this morning but should instead exercise?

You heard this correctly.

An encounter of a prolonged and focused conversation with the brother/teacher that came after many weeks of fearful encounters finally occurred. It came at a time after the crisis of confrontation in the relationship and it seemed to have been a turning point of some kind for me. Even though difficult for my little ego it is like it opened me up. To what I do not know but things are different somehow. Not just with the relationship with this particular person but in general and in my sense of expectation and change.

You were ready for this lesson/healing. After the many weeks of low-level interactions that were full of your floating fear you were able to in effect say, "Okay, whatever is to come, I am ready." The time was partly needed by your brother who with you is processing this energy of fear. And yes, you were able to see the Christ in your brother. Yes you felt it in your gut. Some of it was your own relief. You properly recognize that getting to the issues allowed you to stop generalizing and thus reduce the fear. Also, your brother was able to do the same thing as it became more focused and manageable in his eyes too.

Is this the sea change You mentioned a little while back? What is it? What behavior has/will indicate it to me?

It is you registering the sea change. It is of your immediate environment first. In the case of this most recent lesson, it is of the relationship with your brother. However, it is also the beginning of the next great shift in consciousness of the entire race.

It is in you and the many others who are beginning to awaken. There is a critical mass that is not yet but is stirring and many there are who "feel" it or register it somehow even if they are not yet overtly aware of it at the level of what you now consider normal waking consciousness. Those of you who are waking up, who are beginning to actually feel it, will be helping to inform and to lead it into manifestation by your very act of registering it even if you do not understand.

It will be known by many indicators. The core shift will be of an attitude manifesting first in individuals then throughout all of humanity.

Look for behavior which is more inclusive. There is much to be known and learned in the last simple sentence.

I did not see this yesterday, this sea change. Or did I?

It was evident in parts of your encounter. However, do not project your own version of what it will or should look like. Each will express it in their own way. Also, the tide will not turn in a day. Many old patterns of behavior will continue. Some will have value in continuing to break down the old patterns which must go. Some will be seen as counterproductive and will present the opportunity to learn.

It seems as though we are buying into the rat race. It seems as though we are losing our center.

You are. This is part of the registering of the perception of the fundamental change or shift that we have called the sea change. It will be a necessary phase. Much good will come of it. You must practice your detachment. You will serve also by sharing joy and being a point of reassurance.

I feel that I did that much better in times past and that now my new level of rapport with You has actually come at a time when I am less involved in the direct interacting that once was so active and occasioned regularly by laughter.

You are becoming more detached. Interactive humor is a way to touch others but is a lower form of bringing joy. Look to one of your favorite phrases, ". . . And the joy we share as we tarry there"[5] is the joy of the higher and is not just funny or hilarious but all pervasive. This you have felt and it stays in your memory precisely because it was of an order of magnitude greater than anything you have known. This is the joy that is of the higher. This is what you are to bring and share. This is the joy that comes with the peace that passeth understanding. This is the joy that liberates. Seek it first and always in yourself. Seek it in your heart for it is there always. When you can tap into it you will then naturally express it and those around you will be able to bathe in its light. In this way you will be a light bearer.

So when I tell you to have joy it means much more than your getting centered; it means your brother also getting his center. In this way your joy will fill the Earth because it will be shared and move one to the other. It will not be your own personal joy but will be the greater joy of the whole. It will be the hallmark of the connectedness of all. There is only One thing. How many times have you yourself said this? Take the proper next step and have the joy of this discovery and share, by your new presence in it, this joy with everyone you meet. It will spill over to those who are in your proximity and who may never actually register your presence in their lower perceptions. But they will feel a lift. They will feel an energizing of their field. This will shorten greatly the time to their own awakening.

You read well <u>A Course In Miracles</u> wherein you found your own response in that you were told that awakening is often into fear. These moccasins you know well. Move on and through it.

I know I have asked before and this narrative is already full of suggestions. However—well, You already know my question even before I ask.

Yes, I do. No, as noted before there is no magic bullet. You must accept to the entire field and know it in its entirety. Connecting to and staying in the joy will be your answer. Roosevelt was right when he said, "The only thing we have to fear is fear itself." It was no accident that you heard that on the radio just yesterday.

As I reread some of our words here I see great beauty in them. I want to move to a place where these can be our focus and not so much my own struggle to deal with my fear and little ego. What I have come to call my Spiritual whining.

We will return to them and you will not be disappointed. However, the work of letting go must also be attended to or the next higher level will not be achievable.

Why is this so damn hard?

Your struggle is that of coming out of a deep sleep when suddenly shocked by a bright light or loud noise. In the shock it is easy to interpret the event with fear. The engrained defense mechanisms are instantly deployed and your first response is that of fight or flight. Both are inappropriate as you are safe where you are. However, lifetimes of the fear response which often appeared to be saving of the physical life has left a set of automatic responses which serve you poorly now. In fact they are counterproductive. You must unlearn them. A way of unlearning them is found in another indicator of the shift or the sea change. That is, the mental power to analyze has developed greatly in the race in only a short time. It is this that is also awakening now, first at lower levels of mental activity and linear mentation. It is also at the same time accelerating at higher levels in what is called intuition.

You know that the sudden bright light is that of your Soul and it comes to bathe you in joy and ultimate protection from all harm. Nothing can harm you. In fact the very light that triggers the old response pattern of fear and fight or flight is the guarantee of safety. Yet your first instinct is to run from the light, to run from safety. This is the instinct of the lower and must be unlearned. You must consciously assert your higher knowledge and act upon it.

It is a volitional event. Thus, it is said that the Universe constantly gives you choices. You get to choose again and again as you perfect your response mechanism so as to get the proper response to become the first response. That response is to remember and reconnect with Me. That response is to be able to recognize when you are not connected and to move to reestablish yourself in the connection. That response is to be in the flow and be the flow.

The serendipity of yesterday was great as I experienced a totally unexpected plane ride and then the meeting of a brother and learning of his connection to me. Thank You.

> The flow is nothing but serendipity. It was but a taste of what will be when you abandon the control and worry of the little ego. You also had many moments of recognizing that you still have fear as it appeared just under the surface from time to time. And you now understand from your reading of A Course In Miracles that the fear or what is called there, discomfort, has a purpose. The purpose is to call you to focus on the higher. Now you can see the anxiety as one of the signs that you asked about. It calls for correction.
>
> A day of rest today is a good idea. Do your exercises, rest, and read, and talk with me.
>
> Return now to Exercise 1 and again visualize, actually see in your creative imagination a new pair of glasses or contact lenses being put into place. These will correct your sight so as to allow you to look through the eyes of your Soul and not through your lower personality, lower mind and little ego. Once the new prescription has been fitted you will have a period of adjustment. However, these optics are not of the kind that you may be used to. They respond to your higher-self but cannot work without your ongoing reinforcement. This will be especially true at first.
>
> Now in the higher mind, the place of gathering wisdom, behold, see, and know that the ongoing reinforcement is part of both your learning and

71

your continuing to give your permission for the correction to take place. Remember that the Father gives you free will. You may, if you wish, continue not to see through the eyes of your Soul and remain with your little ego visions. However, by being constantly aware of the change that you have asked for, you provide reinforcement by giving your permission and you gain reinforcement through the practice and the new view of the Universe. Behold the way of learning the higher and begin to grow also in wisdom.

The new universal view will bring you a new set of perspectives from higher levels and will allow you to test these new ways of looking and seeing. The testing is up to you. Hierarchy does not ask for blind acceptance of anything. A thoughtful review of each new venue is always appropriate. This is so that you will establish a truth that is your own. You should not blindly accept or fail to interpret the new knowledge that will come to you. Such is the nature of free will.

Also remember, however, that the Father does not give you the right to opt out. Thus the knowledge in A Course In Miracles and the other wisdom that we will share here are part of the required course(s) of all. You may say no, not now. But, you may not say no, not ever. You may choose how you see, interpret, and utilize the perspectives that come to you. This includes rejecting those that do not meet your current need for a certain version of reality. However, you may not not grow. The very essence of creation is to grow. This is in your genes, mind, heart, and Soul. It is pandemic in all of Creation because it is all of Creation. You may choose when and how to go with this program. You may not however, postpone it indefinitely nor dishonor its process.

A life will come to every being within which, in the case in point, you will hear the call to begin dealing in earnest with the required growth. A life will come when you will start to see some of the higher perspectives and they will leave you dissatisfied with those of the lower.

First, experiences will occur which do not match your version of reality. New values will awaken and in order to deal with them you will need a new set of mechanisms with which to express them. The old ways will lose their satisfactions—lose their grip. And you will find yourself in the midst of a tug of war between the things of the lower, the battleground of the little personality driven ego, and the things of the Soul, the playground.

It is truly said, "It's all about Soul".[6] This is where you are at this moment.

These glimpses of the higher knowing leave you forever dissatisfied with the lower. You begin to entertain the idea that the things of the lower may actually not be at all but may be instead illusion. However, the illusion is powerful for it has been created by the little ego to be a complete universe unto itself and is designed to keep the little ego in power. Every aspect is progressively linked to every other in such a way that until you begin to see from another perspective altogether, you will not see a unified field that answers every objection about its validity.

The little ego wants you to never mind that its universe is upside down and inside out. Never mind that this ego created universe is replete with its own rationalizing away of anything that does not fit. You are told that it is real and in the ultimate upside-downness you are held hostage to the understanding that if you can't or won't see the reality of this inherently insane perspective, then you will be judged insane.

It is a wonderful trap because from the view of the little ego it is not a trap at all but real. It is seen as self-starting and self-stopping and self-fulfilling. It is its own reward and all you must do in order to render it ongoing is deny the blatant inconsistencies that puncture it daily.

When you do succeed in getting glimpses of the higher reality and begin to act with new mechanisms to deal with that higher reality, the little ego does the only thing it knows to do to cope with denial of its denial and that is to attack. In this case, it attacks itself. The result is pain in the form of conflict, anxiety, and fear. The little ego is literally scared to death because to lose its hold is, in its eyes (the very sight that you are about correcting), to cease to be, to die. It does not want to see, will not see that it can grow into a higher level of consciousness and become One with the greater thing that its universal view has allowed it to declare itself to be, but which is unsustainable in your growing awakening in the light of compounding inconsistencies.

Inconsistencies such as death and other miracles mar the universe of the little ego. Its response is denial. Here too is evidence of the inside out nature of its world view. If it just is not there then everything can remain corralled. However, this position cannot be sustained and thus the turmoil which we see today. The old ways are no longer working. Everything is in change. The change is in direct proportion to that needed to shake the hold of this universal view as promulgated by the little ego. This is because the little ego has done what it was supposed to do.

Lest we be guilty of using the strategy of attack of the little personality, the little ego, we need to keep in perspective the very important developmental work that has been done. A point in evolution is reached where a strong personality is essential to being able to progress on the Spiritual path. The little ego is the result of lifetimes of development of this needed personality. To the extent that such ego development has been accomplished, the individual is ready to move on. However, the very personality needed for the progress on the path is the thing retarding one's growth at this point as that personality, in order to become strong enough to move on to higher levels of integration, has had to pass through an egocentric phase. This egocentric phase which reinforces the perception of separation was necessary for the individuation of itself. However, the time when this was useful has past.

It is now the time of unity, sharing, and the rising of the consciousness of the group. It is truly said that man must now come out of the herd and join the group. In order to do that he must pass through a period where he sees himself as apart from, separate from the herd. To move forward now he must willingly join the group. It must be a volitional act for only in this way will he maintain his individual identity so as to be able to function as an autonomous, fully aware, cooperating, and yet distinct member of the whole.

The little ego has therefore done its job to this point as we are coming into a time when many, many of your brothers are showing signs of stirring and awakening. A strong ego is necessary to this effort. The problem is that the strength of the little ego is also its weakness. In order to grow it has had to have the illusions of the lower mind and has created the phenomenal world within which it believes, and will deny anything to the contrary, that it is supreme. When called upon to grow into a higher level of integration then, it sees that as loss of its specialness and denies the call; or when you, evolving into greater Soul contact, begin to hear the call, it attacks with visions of fear, and calamity.

So be gentle with your little ego. It is a frightened child whose cry is really a call for help. But, like your being awakened by a sudden loud noise or bright light, it may well perceive help as attack.

You yourself once wrote, "You, like a sudden early spring, surprising me with joy, run barefoot through my mind."

As above, so below.

PART SIX

WE ARE ONE, EVER

I, at times, observe in those around me a tension and almost desperate despair as if the sheer pressure of this time of great change is such that they may lose any positive and hopeful perspective. It seems at times that I can sense it in strangers I meet or simply come into proximity with such as when walking through an airport. At such times it comes to me to reassure them somehow and I find myself telling them mentally or occasionally in conversation that all will be well.

> Yes, by all means tell them that all will be well, that all manner of thing will be well. They will respond. They are eager for leadership and someone to make sense of the chaos they see and fear.
>
> You have also correctly observed a new level of urgency among your brothers. There is a sense of running out of time. View this through the compassion of your love/wisdom.

It is joyous. What an extraordinary thing! Our last talk was very reinforcing. Thank You. I am getting the hang of this. I also am able to see the bigger picture and have moments of clear impatience to be on with it. As is suggested in <u>A Course In Miracles</u>, I want to shorten the time.

It also says in <u>A Course In Miracles</u> that once you have connected to Spirit that miracle working is no longer needed. Can You help me with this one as I have been thinking that I need to pursue the skills for becoming a miracle worker?

> You are not yet at the level where the Spirit's original state of direct communication has been reached. You are there sometimes and then not focused at others. However, you have and you are pursuing those skills. You are working miracles. You have seen them. When you connect to Spirit you have begun to work them consciously. Thus, the placement of yourself as miracle worker is enhanced and you are no longer just a gate but a conscious point of focus. You now can, at times, reach the level of function which permits you to volitionally target and direct the energy of love.
>
> This is a responsibility as well as a privilege. It has permitted you to work with groups as well as individuals. It is your power to empower. In practical terms it means that you can now see the opportunity and act with awareness. This is why you were told that you would get better at seeing your brother's need and readiness.
>
> Here you must be careful to have yourself ready to give only the higher energy. For you do not know how it will be utilized. Once you have energized your brother, the energy will move on to others and so needs to be as high and as pure as you can make it. Your detachment is necessary here for

you do not have the level to see how to influence the energy's travel and utilization. Leave this to Me and the Masters. If you should try to influence this you may undo the good because you do not yet see enough of the Plan.

Your test and task is to make sure that your motivation is always from the highest level lest your little ego level needs confuse you. This would result in your trying to use your power to wrongly influence events and your brothers directly. "Be always sure you're right-then go ahead."[7] is sound advice. In this case it means right-minded. See that your motive is always for the higher and greater good and never to aggrandize the little self. See to it that you give freely, honestly and with love to all that you meet. Neither give to influence them nor withhold in order to influence them or events. You simply do not know what you are doing at higher levels of the Plan. However, when you serve in this way with detachment you need only know that you are serving. The Masters will do the rest. And the Masters are grateful and in need of your service. Your detachment is part of your gift to them.

As for your communicating with Me, you haven't seen anything yet. Open up and ask. I will appear without a doubt in your eyes of wonder.

You will have more joy than that which you can now conceive. You will have more joy than you could now handle. However, it will be soon and you can shorten the time even further by your choices, service and awareness in each moment. Continue to wake up. Do so with awareness moment to moment. Put a metaphorical finger in the wind and plumb the flow and then go with it and stay with it. The gain will be everything. The loss will be no-thing.

"Open up and ask," You say. Let me try and report what I have learned. My immediate task is to practice being conscious of the connection and thereby making the connection. I am to focus and refocus throughout the day analogous to Transmission Meditation. This will allow me to first connect then to remain connected. Further, when connected, I am to look for the Christ in all and consciously send them love and to look for their readiness to receive or "make the turn" and assist them then with directed energy. And when they ask for help in the form of attack, I am to forgive and see the attack for what it is and turn the energy of their attack into love and help for them. Do I have this correct so far?

> That is basically it to start. Of course, as you build on this work the opportunities to practice will grow and so will your inventory of capacities with which to help your brothers awaken. As your capacities grow, you will be given more specific responsibilities commensurate with your ability. It will be fun. It will grow in fascination as you begin to see it unfolding before your eyes.

> Remember to detach. Preservation of your ability to do the work rests on your being detached. Your growth in the work rests on this also. When you are attached, you are not growing.

The implication is that I will be progressively more able to hear Your voice as You speak to me.

This is true.

Is there something more I can do to strengthen and enhance that process so as to have it, Your voice, louder, more clear and definite?

> Sure, clear away the distractions. Deny the illusion that there is actually anything causing the interference. Use denial as it was intended and deny that there is interference of any kind. Say to yourself that you and I are One. Know that I am closer than your hand. See Me as surrounding you, enfolding you, encasing you, and holding you. I am not only the glow of the light that you can now see outlining your physical body but I am also the light that is in your heart. There is no place even unto the ends of the Earth and beyond where or when we are not One. I am one with the One in whom you live and move and have your being. And I love you dearly. It is unnatural then when you do not see and commune with Me. The natural state is to focus on the connection and to simply know that it is there. Resting in the knowledge and being secure in the connection is the most natural thing in the world. To do anything else is unnatural and is to have the connection wrested from you. With it goes peace.
>
> Do not settle for anything less than all there is. Want all there is. Little ego needs are illusions. You pursue them at the expense of all there is. To have your lower desires is to be cut off from all there is.
>
> The peace of God is all there is.

It takes real effort to move away from the peace of God and to sustain the disconnection. You must fight to stay disconnected. It requires constant maintenance and constant conflict to keep the perspective of separation. The energy level needed for this effort is such that you have nothing left for your brother. The illusion is that to be separate is the natural state and as you cling to this it actually takes more and more energy because the Universe is calling you to unity all the time and giving you signals and signs at every moment. It requires more and more effort to ignore these signs and signals as they multiply daily.

All this will lead all to say at some point that there has to be a better way. The purpose of the conflict then is to be a learning environment within which you can keep choosing until you see not just the absurdity of the choices but the absurdity of choosing anything but the peace of God. When this point is reached, you begin to reset the parameters to look for choices outside of the box you think you are in. The purpose of the conflict is to get your attention. The purpose of the conflict is to shake you up and wake you up. The awakening is to your natural state of awareness of being ever and always in the peace of God.

Thus it is an axiom of the Ageless Wisdom that you get harmony through conflict.

Why am I so tired this morning and last night?

Exercise will help. Also, you put a great deal of energy into the meetings of yesterday, especially the last one. The funeral was also stressful for you. Detachment will help you there. It will help in everything.

Learn to recognize the patterns and cycles of your own energy flow. They are part of the greater cycles. To the extent that you recognize them you can begin to see how to better harmonize with and go with the flow of the greater cycles. There are times when you will require more rest. There are times when you will have more physical energy. As you connect more and learn to sense these patterns, their effects will level out and you will be able to use them within the context of your greater growth.

Remember that there is a greater Plan with its own great cycles. You are part of that. You cannot help being moved by the changes of energy flow in the cosmos. These cosmic energy flows are macro-text for the energy movements at all levels of energy down to the smallest unit of energy.

Everything is connected and all is energy. There is nothing but energy. There is only one great energy field. As you become more connected to it you sense the movement of energy through the field; you sense your own immediate field and its relational aspects to the greater field.

Everything has a vibrational rate. The rate distinguishes levels of density. All vibrations are set within a great harmonic field. So, all is energy and can be differentiated by a continuum of vibration. This energy is Spirit. Matter is vibrating at a low level and is thus dense. Spirit is vibrating at a high level and is thus lighter. As described in many places in the Wisdom teachings, Spirit is matter vibrating at its highest frequency and matter is Spirit vibrating at its lowest frequency. Humanity represents a point of meeting of these vibratory elements in that humankind is in both the world of physical matter and the world of Spirit. However, it is all one continuum. There is no break in the progression from the lower vibration through the highest. They match and form a single harmonic. The apparent duality is in reality, a unity: The Unity of all things.

It is this that is the song celestial that is now being heard increasingly by all of you. It is the song of at-one-ment or atonement.

Herein also is the essence of the becoming of and the actual divinity of humankind. Remember that the One you have come to know, love and look to as a Master taught "I and my Father are one."[8] And, then to those who would stone him for blasphemy, confirmed the law: "Is it not written in your law, I said, Ye are gods"?[9]

After a period of what I thought was much improved understanding and even comradery, the brother with whom I have had such difficulty has chosen again to attack. This time it came in a letter.

You already know the answers. This brother is a teacher for you. The written attack was partially a return to the state of the earlier attack. It was from fear. It was a gift to you in that it is the perfect opportunity to practice detachment and to learn the lessons of your own specialness. It was a cry for help in the form of attack. It "gets" to you because it threatens you so directly at the ego level because you think you have something to lose.

I have been told that I am in the right place. Is this still true?

Always and forever you are in the right place as you are in your Father's house. However, what you are really asking is about this particular geographical place, this particular job, and this particular group of brothers. The answer is yes. Again, you knew that.

This last attack allowed you also to think of your detachment in terms of how it works. This then has been a good lesson in furthering your understanding.

Also, remember that as your sense of service blossoms you must integrate into your knowing the need to serve all. This includes those who may appear to be less focused in the reality of their own Spirit.

You do tend to over empathize with the specialness concerns of the ego of those you deal with. Look for balance here lest you become too removed and use it as an excuse not to care. Also remember to be detached is not the same as not caring.

Is this part of "What you think of as the future will soon be the past"? And if so, can You tell me more about what those changes will be? Is it only my perception of the future or for all?

Yes, this is your seeing the call for you to shift your view away from that of reliance on the specialness of the little ego to the detachment of the Soul. The great struggle that you see in your brother is also yours, meaning all of humanities' at this time.

When the vision is shifted, by definition, the future will not, may not, look like the past. The shift must first be yours. You have your new prescription fitted. Recall also that shortly after beginning the work with Exercise 1 that you were fitted with a new prescription for your physical glasses and that you experienced an energy and impression of a relationship between those new glasses and the results of your creative imaging work of getting a new Spiritual pair in the exercise. Thus, you have also had an overshadowing experience of your new physical glasses as well. As above so below: There are no accidents.

I was able to wait a day before trying to talk to the brother who wrote the letter of attack. It proved a very difficult conversation. However, it had a very subtle but different quality compared to the last conversations following the episodes of attack not long ago. It seemed as though there were some words and unrelated events that had new meaning almost as if they were meant as a signal. One of the events was the passing of an emergency vehicle with its siren sounding and which even in the difficulty of the moment registered as an event that had bearing or meaning for the conversation we were in.

You had here, embedded in the encounter, many mini lessons of just how and what you think of as the future will soon be the past. You are never without guidance and the call to return to your heart. This is true even when you may be in the midst of feeling attack or making attack. It is the song celestial and it runs under every moment, event, happening, encounter, conversation, or thought. It plays always for you as a beacon, guide, talisman, and way to see truth and Me. In this case the very landmarks, the signs and signals were given to you right within the context of the actual words of the conversation itself. This is the way it works. It is always there for you and requires only that you see it and then act on the opportunity to return your focus to the higher, the connection that you are trying now to learn to get and keep. It is a guide to remembering, that is to re-membering.

It is a wake-up call. It is your own fear of the change which is coming. It lets you see the fear of your brothers and to be better prepared and understanding when they, like you, even if only in your mind and fantasy, attack.

The observation of the sound of the siren was such a wake-up call in the midst of your discussion. It was a pointed reminder not to indulge support and validation of the little ego with its sense of specialness. It was also an opportunity to receive guidance not to suggest the issue of specialness or allude to examples of this type of behavior as you perceived him to be demonstrating in that moment. Not that particular brother, not then. It would have been misunderstood, viewed as attack by you and registered in the ego as hurtful. You correctly used that signpost to hold the thought from being manifest into speech and thus had a lesson in the law of occult silence.

> You have also been able to recognize the time it has taken you to return to a more centered state. You have looked into the process and not just reacted to it. This shows your growth. Your challenge now is to move on to the point where the detachment is more readily the first response.

> Nothing can harm you. All will be well.

In my study of the Ageless Wisdom literature I have read of the law of occult silence. With the word "occult" meaning simply hidden or unrevealed, I understand the law to mean that one does not try to share certain things or to teach them until you know that the brother is ready because to do so could cause that person to experience fear or confusion.

> Like all such concepts there are many layers of meaning to be learned in the abstract and then mastered in practice. You have the essence correct. As in any opportunity to help a brother, your first obligation is to do no harm. This is why we are spending much time on the lesson of detachment. Remember detachment does not mean that you do not care. In the case of the law of silence, it is an opportunity to learn of your great love for your brother such that you withhold speech that would not serve him.

But when the fear comes it is so hard to hear Your voice and to remember to ask for help and to establish or reestablish the connection.

> Yet, you have asked, even in this encounter with

this brother, who is at this time a great teacher for you, in the midst of the fear and anxiety. So the first step is becoming available to your own recall. The next must be to place detachment at the forefront. Then you will not be disconnected in the first place and will not have to reconnect in an effort to hear My voice.

I have recently come upon a suggestion that using an actual image in my mind of kindness is a good tool when working to focus myself to higher levels. Is this appropriate to the context of seeing my brother with love?

> The little ego will take any concept as an opportunity to indulge specialness, even efforts by you at what you think of as Spiritual growth. You must examine your own motive. When it is part of your illusion of specialness, it is not a true kindness and compassion. When it is part of your little ego self-image, you are using it as validation of that little ego and a point of comparison allowing you to determine superiority relative to the response of your brother, when in reality you are not better than him and to judge him in any way is error. Heal this in yourself and heal it in him, who is your brother, in all brothers and sisters.

Busted! Lord these are hard sayings!

> The shortest way through is the truth. You would not now be asking if you were not ready to hear it.

Thank You. I must ask again then, am I in the right place?

> The gift of reaching the point where you can with volition talk with Me is the gift of asking. This includes asking again and again for in each question is the opportunity not just for repetition, a good thing, but also for deeper meanings to be revealed.
>
> So, yes you are in the right place and all will yet be well. Moves will come. You know that now because you begin to understand that change is part of the Plan of the Creator. It is the way of allowing and when necessary compelling your growth. This will at times involve geographic changes but most of the time will involve relationship evolutions and what you think of as people coming and going in your life. Relationship is the quintessential training ground and the ultimate playground.
>
> Some of your frustration and disappointment, both of these are ultimately of the ego, is from the wish that your brothers would act more like the few who are awakened and in whom you see the promise of the great future that is ahead. You are impatient as you hold this high ideal of how people should relate. It is a noble vision given to you over many lives of your own trial and error coupled with your growing understandings of reality. However, your higher vision of organic empowerment is not yet possible. More of the old forms are yet to be removed. You do not see them in this way as yet. Your sight is improving but you do not see enough of the Plan yet to give you the confidence of that knowledge. Thus, faith will be needed. The faith of

a Moses or a Gandhi is what you need to develop. They did not see the full picture but still answered when called to act.

You have climbed enough mountains for now. Let this be the one upon which you stop climbing, rest and do the work.

PART SEVEN

HONESTY OF MIND, SINCERITY OF SPIRIT, AND DETACHMENT

The Great Lord in His role as World Teacher has given a practice to aid all in the acquisition and sustaining of higher awareness. He has said to cultivate "honesty of mind, sincerity of Spirit, and detachment."

You have already here explanation of detachment.

Honesty of mind is just that. "To thine own self be true."[10] This is because the separation is not an actual separation but the splitting of the mind into fragmented parts of lower, of the ego, and higher, of the Spirit. It is not uncommon for you to have one thought at one level of mind and its opposite at another level. Honesty of mind will help to heal this rift by requiring that you think the same thoughts to yourself at all levels. You do this with your watch on what you think.

To practice honesty of mind first become aware of what you think. Actually "see" your thoughts and examine them for consistency. Are they worthy of a loving Son of God? If not, rethink them. Correct the error, whatever it is, and move on. Do not fall into the trap of guilt set by the little ego. You are called upon to be totally forgiving of others. Be as forgiving of yourself as you are of them. Hold nothing against your brother and so hold nothing against yourself. By rethinking you can actually cancel out erroneous thoughts before they become more powerful thought-forms. Heal them with love as you are urged to heal your brother and his thoughts with love.

Sincerity of Spirit means to be, at whatever level you can, about the work of the Spirit. It means to know that the purpose of your earthly sojourn is to learn and grow strong in the Spirit. That is, in the connection to the Spirit and to become One with that Spirit. It means to do this with purpose, direction and understanding and be about it first and not as an afterthought. Sincerity of Spirit will create and maintain right-mindedness.

Reviewing our last several weeks I note that so very, very much of what You say is about the need to develop detachment. May we go into this more, please? Can You give me a working definition and suggestions for achieving detachment?

It is said so very, very much because it is the lesson you need so now. It is good that you wish to look more deeply at detachment, it is a powerful tool.

Detachment comes with the connectedness. Detachment is the result of looking for what is really there and beyond the illusion of the lower world. This is why you have been fitted with a new prescription so as to correct the physical sight, which sees only the things that bind you. Detachment is a perspective of pure love within which you see your brother as the perfect being that he is. You see him as he was created and you know from what you see that he is not capable of harming you or himself or anyone. Detachment is the natural state. Attachment to the things of the lower is the unnatural state and indicates specialness and the acceptance of the illusion of separation.

Detachment is recognizing error for what it is and correcting it through true forgiveness. Detachment is keeping your head even in the midst of the storm as others are losing theirs, for detachment lets you see that there is no storm. It is the capacity to see, get above, and let go of the things of the lower.

Detachment, once achieved makes you a natural healer and teacher to your brother whose own detachment is requisite to the unfolding of the Plan.

Detachment is being in the world and yet not of the world.

Detachment is seeing what the Holy Spirit sees, which is the Christ within all brothers and the Unity of all Creation. It is the capacity to see the love that underlies all things and the joy of the union and reunion of those so loved. It is the looking past the error of your brother to his heart in which you see the same spark of the Divine that is in you and all others.

Detachment is the achieving of a certain perspective whereby you observe events unfolding without reacting to them as if they are real within the rules made by the lower world, but can see them as the illusion that they are and can respond to them not from the lower but the higher. It is being in the flow and being the flow.

Detachment is not not caring. It is the opposite. Remember that the world of the little ego is upside down, inside out and backward. Those who see detachment as not caring are reacting from this perspective. Detachment is a true act of love in that it permits you to look past the error of your brother and it positions you to serve with love by healing yourself and your brother.

It is only from a point of detachment that you can see the attack behavior of your brother as the cry for help that it is. Detachment lets you see the battleground from above where it is seen in its true light as the playground.

You achieve detachment by looking through your new eyes. You achieve detachment by actually seeing the world differently. To achieve detachment, look always first for the Christ in your brother. This will render all other things into their proper perspective.

To achieve detachment, recognize error for what it is. It is just an error. It is not sin. It is not the mark of a being that is worthy of attack. It is not an indicator that the one making the error is unworthy in any way, no matter what the error. It is after all, only a failure to see.

95

It is seeing for yourself the absurdity of the box that you think you are in and declaring that there must be a better way. It is the shifting to that better way. This is done instantly and occurs whenever any brother gets the perspective of detachment if only for a moment.

As the Master has indicated, there are three foundational perspectives needed for spiritual growth: honesty of mind, sincerity of spirit, and detachment.

To be so detached is to gift this world with another voice, another set of willing hands, another step on the path and another awakened One who realizes his privilege to serve in the awakening of all others.

How many times have you observed that a movie plot begins by establishing the behavior of someone or ones as unspeakably bad thus to engender the judgment that they are worthy of attack? This is always the basis of the revenge type plot. To be detached is to see the set up as inherently erroneous and to see the whole thing within the greater context of the falsity of the premise of separation and specialness. Of course, this tends to cost you the entertainment value of such things. However, your gain is always infinitely greater than the false perception of the loss because the gain is to see the Universe as God created it and not the world of fear and revenge as the little ego desires to remake it. The gain is to have the peace of God, your natural state and the gift of God that is built into all Creation.

These and all such movie plots are but reflecting the acceptance of and reinforcement of the little ego view that separation is real. By achieving detachment, you see that this is not so and that reality comes only from recognition of the unity of all things and the brotherhood of all beings.

There is only One thing. In all of Creation, there is only One thing. It is a single living, breathing, growing, unified whole that is in its completeness, Holy. However, when that completeness is denied by the little ego, it does not impact the integrity of the Creation in any way. That integration remains intact and unchangeable. What has changed is the ability to sense, see, and otherwise to perceive, to know Oneness with that integrity. When that completeness is denied, one becomes attached to the illusion and this is an error of perception only and does not constitute grounds nor permission to annihilate, either in word, thought or deed, your brother. As you have said many times, Adolph Hitler went to heaven.

To achieve detachment, you must only let go. The little ego wants to control in the mistaken belief that it actually can. The little ego suffers from the delusion that if only enough control can be gained then it can have all its desires met. The inherent problem with this view is that to control at this level is to do so at the perceived direct expense of other little egos with exactly the same agenda, thus, the conflict. Detachment allows one to transcend this dilemma and to give control of the Universe back to the Creator where it not only belongs but where it has always been. The control of the little ego exists within the context of its mistaken belief that the little ego can actually gain control. To do this, it has made a world of separation, opposition, and competition. It chooses to see only separately in order to have a basis to strive for its needs of specialness. The little ego thus has chosen not to see the reality of the unity of all things. Detachment breaks the hold of the little ego. When one is detached one can look beyond the lower, be patient with the unfolding, and become an agent for serving and awakening others.

Detachment is seeing with true vision. Detachment is true love for all your brothers in the knowledge that to help them you must be able to look beyond their desire and see their need. Detachment is the power to not get caught up in the stampede. It is the ability to see the herd and not run with it but to intelligently move into the group. Detachment lets you be flexible knowing that one way or another, the Plan will unfold and that it is for the perfect good of all your brothers and sisters.

Detachment is requisite to connectedness.

Look first for the Christ in your brother. This will mean that you are looking not for evidence to sustain specialness. When you look first for the Christ, you are by definition looking above and beyond the world made by the little ego. When you take your eye off of the goal, what you see are obstacles. In the case of the little ego's world, the obstacles are the seductive elements of separation and specialness and competition. The world made by the little ego is completed by denial that anything else exists. "He knoweth not that he knoweth not" is rendered complete and whole in the world of the little ego by the refusal to know. Detachment allows one to know that he does not know which is the beginning of wisdom.

To be detached, you must adopt the position of the observer. It is not, however, a position of uncaring. The detached observer looks at the whole scene and does not buy into its parts. The detached observer can see context, history, and desire as well as the love and spark of God brought by all brothers to any happening. Detachment allows the observer to position for this broad perspective and to then train himself to select for the higher in his brother and thus himself.

It is the position of the loving brother watching his beloved siblings. It is the parent who lets the child go out to play but keeps a watch ready to assist when the child needs help but not participating directly in the child's reality. And thus, not buying into the values of the child's games but selectively reinforcing those values which lead to growth. It is seeing the playground.

Detachment requires first a conscious effort. One must know that one is able to do this and then by an act of will, do it. Detachment requires practice in order to break old patterns well established by the little ego which, when deferred to, will always respond within the context of separation, specialness and competition. Detachment then is a mighty first step and powerful tool for breaking the grip of the apparent realness of the world made by the little ego. It provides the way to turn the world made by the little ego back outside out and upside up thus restoring to the vision the capacity to see the real world of the Creator.

To observe from this perspective is to grow yourself because you learn from your brother. He brings you opportunity after opportunity to see the infinite number of ways in which the little ego couches its justifications and to decide to see them, that is to choose to see them, as the illusion they are or, to choose to buy into them. This is your brother's gift to you.

I experienced yesterday some general anxiety. Was this related to or mostly nutritional?

Nutrition was and is a significant part as were the machinations of the little ego as it contemplates its knowing that it can't go back and its fear of what is ahead.

Any suggestions on how to better handle those times and to avoid them altogether?

You will grow in this regard. You are growing.

As for the nutritional part learn to observe sooner the signs and eat the right food sooner. However, as the stress fades more, this too will improve the body reactions.

Practice your connectedness. Learn to stay in conscious link. Remember that the link is always there as I am always here. Yours is to re-member and thus to reconnect.

Yes, these times are moments of what is oft referred to as the dark night of the Soul.

This activity, this writing, this *journal of a student* has displaced my meditation time. Given the strong and consistent call to meditation that is found in the Ageless Wisdom teachings, is this a problem?

Your meditation has changed. It has not stopped. Recall your activity of yesterday when you were at prayer frequently throughout the day. Remember also our conversation off and on throughout the day. Even though you had difficulty sustaining it, that was a conversation of meditation. One of the points of meditation is to provide for the regular effort at Soul contact. Is this not what you are doing at this moment?

This activity, coupled with the more focused service done regularly in the group, will be a good pattern for a while. The conscious addition of moments of specific contact, or short little catch-up times with Me at specific intervals during the day, are also a good idea. These could take the form of a few minutes at lunch and even during a bathroom break. This time will help even though, especially given your concerns right now about demonstrating work time on task, it might appear to be a distraction. However, these few minutes taken to reconnect will allow your work to flow from the higher point of the connectedness. This will have the impact of improving the effectiveness and timeliness of all your life, and work will improve in effectiveness and purpose. This is not to say that your times of contact should not come in your more traditional meditation practice.

Remember the whole point of meditation is to promote this very contact. As noted earlier, the time will come when your connectedness will be such that your being unconnected will be the exception. So practice all you can in whatever ways you can and expand your definition of what is meditation. Ultimately any effort aimed at connecting with Me is meditation.

Just prior to sitting down to write this morning, I discovered a cricket had gotten into the house. I did not wish it any harm and so placed a small bowl over it which will hold it in place and allow me to return it to the outside when we are through this morning. I am now sitting here feeling guilty about imprisoning the cricket even though my intentions are to free it soon. What should I do?

Go and let him out.

I was told in our conversation of yesterday that a significant part of my difficulty with fear and anxiety of the day before was due to my getting off the diet.

Your system is not yet returned to the point where it can be so shocked and not respond in the way you experienced. Underlying this is the need to integrate your bodies so that you begin to see them and their functioning as a unit with each part interdependent on the other. So, while you have been told to refocus your looking onto the things of the higher and to move away from the illusion that you are the physical body, attention to how the body is fitted into the greater whole is needed. Taking the body totally for granted is not a good idea. A balance here, which acknowledges the needs of the body and provides for its maintenance, must be struck. However, as also noted before, the body is a poor master. In fact the body is simply not capable of such and when you defer to it so as to identify who you are by your body, you lose sight of the things that are real.

Body identification is a tempting illusion and is used by the little ego to reinforce its position of control. This is easily done until one begins to understand that the body is but a learning tool provided by the Creator so as to expedite the lessons to be learned in dense matter. It also has the function of providing vehicle for the Spiritualization of matter. Here the wonder of the body is truly amazing and a blessing. But it is still a functional object and not who you are. Buying into the belief that you are the body is another way of tying you to the illusions of separateness.

The body evolves from incarnation to incarnation and also within each incarnation. As the cells of the body die and are replaced with new ones there is the opportunity to have the next succeeding cell be of a higher vibration and quality each time. This will be a function of many things with proper nutrition, rest, and the impact of the other bodies all being variables in the equation. Periods of stress are less conducive to gain in the quality of body evolution at the cellular level.

The ultimate point is reached when one can control the process at will. This point comes late in that part of the evolutionary process which is completed on the material plane and is characterized by the cells becoming light. This is meant literally. The stuff of which the cells are made becomes light matter. This is what is going on all the time, slowly. When this stage is completed one can demonstrate full control on and over the material plane. One has become a Master.

To become a Master is to finish the stage of evolution which is associated with the need to incarnate on the material plane. One is then freed from the pull of the desires of the lower and goes on to other levels of growth.

Some of this is redundant to my understanding of the Ageless Wisdom material. Are You stating it here for the benefit of those who will read this later?

Correct: Some of this is work that you can do from your previous studies and requires less direct energy from Me. That does not mean that I am not here and in communion with you. It is an example of the continuum of thought and energy. We are One. Where the information has been previously communicated it is not necessary for Me to restate it but is appropriate that it be recalled from your level. This is an example of the disciple contributing directly and parallels that of the contributions of other levels. You thus gain the insight of how each brother learns to contribute what he can and thus grow in the work of unfolding the Plan. This is what goes on at all levels from probationary disciple through Master and beyond. As above, so below.

A brother at work has made an error and done something inappropriate. A second brother, one who has significant authority based power wishes to direct me to use attack to deal with the error. As I reflect on my lessons over the past many, many years this is a common position I have found myself in. So, the admonition to see it as an opportunity to practice detachment and to serve both brothers, whose conflict I am also in, are repetitive themes and clues to lessons as yet to be mastered by me.

> A troubled brother needs your help. You are beginning to see that the help may need to be in the form of attention getting.

My impression from the supervisor brother is that I am being called upon to attack. This is a dilemma.

> The duality of the lower always appears as dilemma. Follow your highest wisdom.

I am asking for that highest wisdom here.

> There are no magic bullets, only your love. A wake-up call is in order for both. It will be up to them to decide how to react. Keep your detachment. You have properly recognized the need for detachment here. Bring the energy of love and be detached. You are never called upon to do anything more or less. Bless them, do your honest best to respond and get out of the way of the higher work. Remember the playground.

How can I play at what is in reality discipline of another.

> It is not so. To bring opportunity for growth is not discipline when done with love. It is instead providing an opportunity for your brother to see the light. That is the difference and it is your challenge

to learn and grow also. Thus your brother brings you the perfect lesson, as he calls for his own.

You are also asking about the material plane consequences to him that you may be called upon to administer. Do whatever is honest and called for with love and not from any lower ego motive. In other words be detached. Then administer what is required within the letter and Spirit of the law unless that law is unjust and against the greater awareness as you now understand it.

PART EIGHT

THE MASTERS OF WISDOM

What is the plan for this journal that will become the book?

> The book is a part of the unfolding of the Plan on earth. It is to help tie together more the lessons given thus far in several sources and is but one of many, many such works aimed at a greater understanding of synthesis and the unity of all things. While much progress has been made in the bringing in of information, there is need for the recognition of the unity of all that has been given. Often the tendency to separateness is a block to continued growth in the wisdom as brothers get new ideas and interpret them as the final truth and stop looking and growing into the progressively greater knowledge that is there and that needs to be grasped if man is to intelligently deal with his current situation. This narrative will deal then with many topics which are familiar but will try to point out how they relate and complement each other so as to contribute to the understanding of the greater synthesis of all knowledge and thus advance the basis for aggregating and properly interpreting that knowledge into wisdom.

As you ask your questions, you provide the opportunity for the information to be so brought forward. Your questions then are your contribution and actually help guide where we go. Do not be concerned that you will not ask the correct question. Here is a lesson: All questions lead to the unfolding of higher truth and wisdom. Just as all roads are part of the greater one road, so all questions are connected and one can and will get to the greater truth of God by asking any question no matter how unrelated it may appear provided that it is followed by another question. This is part of the Plan of the Creator. This is one of the great wonders of Creation. It is built in and works every time. What is needed is the giving of direction to this natural mechanism so as to shorten the time it takes to go from seemingly unrelated or innocuous points through questions to knowledge and wisdom. This guidance is always there. It is closer than your hand. It is in you and it will come out to help you. Expressions of this guidance are found in all of the great works. They contain truth.

The pattern of the unfolding of the truth is now a well-developed one. Truth is promulgated and given through the Hierarchy of the Masters to a brother and passed thus into the pool of knowledge. This is received by man and assimilated into the existing knowledge. This assimilation process is first seen as in opposition to the current or prevailing truth, whatever it is. From the conflict comes a certain degree of harmony as the new knowledge with its apparently new version of reality grows in acceptance. However, the growing in acceptance is accompanied by a distancing from the core of the truth into structures, concepts, dogmas, etc., which progressively define the unfolding in exclusive ways and attempt to make this exclusive interpretation the truth, the whole truth and nothing but the truth defined by its opposition and exclusivity relative to "other" dogmas seen as wrong or misguided. This pattern is an old one and marks the great capacity that man has to cling to separateness and demand that his particular version of the unfoldment be special and convey to him exclusivity. The wars fought in the name of religion are but extensions of this pattern.

There is need then to continually remind you of the unity of all things and that all bodies of knowledge contain the germ of the greater truth. The ability to see with understanding and to know the truth inherent in all doctrines is much needed as a way to break down the barriers of separation. It is more than just tolerating the various beliefs of your brother. It is honoring those beliefs as part of the greater whole and seeing at their essential core level that they express the higher truth and in real terms they are but your own.

To do this is to move out of the herd and into the group.

It is this movement that is needed now. The need is great. The need is urgent. The Plan of God provides for arrival of the next unfoldment just in time to both help in the breaking down of the old and crystallized forms of previous dispensations as well as the creation of the next synthesis of understandings into the next level of knowing. This is what is meant by the turn of the spiral for the resulting gain in understanding is above that of what was and is a step up in the evolution of man's ability both to have the new understandings and also his ability to progressively tap higher levels of these insights. Thus the evolution proceeds.

The juncture is critical now. Man reaches these points from time to time and at each point struggles around the great issues needing resolution that are brought to a focus so as to precipitate the needed growth. Growth in the understanding of the essential unity of all things is what is needed now. The unity principal is to be a significant item in the next great unfoldment. Man must recognize his essential unity as a member of the family of God. He must see that things are at the point where separation and specialness threaten his continued existence on the material plane. Man must learn to embrace his brother's need as his own, for that it is.

And of myself as a being and the Masters of Wisdom?

First, know that we are all One and that everywhere you look there is nothing but God. There exists only an infinite continuum of consciousness differentiated into distinct points of awareness. Each of these points of awareness has specific identity which is achieved at some juncture in the evolutionary process and which grows into ever greater awareness and consciousness of itself and in so doing takes on progressively the characteristics of the Creator. Once attained, this identity is never lost.

Masters are those who have moved through the part of the process requiring incarnation or human experience. All life in this Universe is either human, on its way to this experience, or has been through this experience. It is a gateway experience and a required course. The Masters, who are now with you and who are re-entering the mass awareness of the race, are those who elected to stay involved with the direct evolution of humanity and have chosen this venue for Their further service. Other venues of service are available upon graduation from the physical level of evolution of what is often referred to as Earth School. To be human is to be on your way to becoming a Master. All will become Masters.

Steps to Masterhood include a series of plateaus called initiations. These are the first five of which the first four are taken on the physical plane level. The fifth may be taken while incarnate, that is during a physical lifetime, but this is not necessary as it is to the first four. Masters have taken these five initiations. Upon completing the fifth, Masterhood has been demonstrated and one is no longer bound by the pull of the material world. You no longer have the desire for the experiences that are possible there.

We will need to do more on the initiations later but for now let us stay with the nature of Masterhood. A Master has full control of all His bodies and over the material plane. A Master has demonstrated this control and is free then of the karma and pull of desire that brings one into incarnation over and over again. They have mastered it. On the way He has experienced all that the lower plane has to offer. Masters have, in Their time in time, been, done, seen, experienced, and grown through all the races and roles of humanity. They have made choice after choice after choice and in so doing have gained the wisdom to choose the higher over the lower. To do this They, like you, and all who read this, have been saint and sinner, teacher and learner, builder and destroyer, lover and hater, servant and served, writer and reader, noble and base, exploiter and exploited, killer and killed. They have lived the life of duality in the world of duality made by the little ego and have risen in Their level of knowledge and consciousness to the point that They see and always choose the higher and are no longer trapped in the lower. Here you and all of your brothers will go also.

To have achieved such mastery is to have reached a level of direct communion with God so that one understands Their essential Unity with all things and expresses nothing but that Unity. One is aware that They are not only in but also of the body of God. In so being They are all Sons of God. Masters are more aware and more able to actualize and to more intensely know and live this truth, moment-to-moment. All are of the Sonship. There was not just one Son. There is only One Son. And the Sonship is One.

To get to mastery one has passed through the lower kingdoms of Earth and moved into the kingdom of Souls. This is the fifth kingdom. The others are the kingdoms of mineral, vegetable, animal, and man or human. Each kingdom is characterized by a progressively higher rate of vibration and thus capacity to sustain greater awareness. Each kingdom grows out of the previous one and is, in turn, dependent upon but also informs and has service to that lower. In the case of man, he has this dependence and service and because of his awareness, also has responsibility for and in this sense, dominion over, all the lower kingdoms of the Earth. But, man is not separate from them. Unity is not only the truth of all Creation but its underlying operational dynamic.

Masters who have chosen to stay and serve the Plan of and on Earth have a relationship to mankind as mankind has to the lower kingdoms: As above, so below.

These Masters have great love and compassion for all of Creation as it unfolds on Earth. By the way, They also have great joy. Masters have wonderful humor and express it naturally with joy and laughter. To be in the presence of a Master is to know joy, laughter, bliss and that all is well and will be well. They see much more of The Plan of God and are dedicated to serving this Plan. Each Master is also lovingly responsible for brothers who are far enough along to be considered disciples. These He teaches. In turn, those disciples who are far enough along take an active role in the teaching of those who are aspirants and probationary disciples. Each level has growing to do and receives help from the next higher level which bears loving responsibility in turn for that next lower level. This is true also of the Masters Themselves. This then is a part of the infinite continuum of consciousness differentiated into distinct points of awareness: As above, so below.

The Masters are organized such that the senior among Them are looked up to for Their greater wisdom. These have greater responsibility. They are thus organized into a Hierarchy and are often referred to in the wisdom literature as the Hierarchy. There is at Their head the great Lord, lovingly acknowledged and joyfully served by Them, the Master of the Masters.

Thus, Masters are your elder brothers. They are Gods in the sense that They are on Their way to ever and ever more intimate awareness of Their Unity with the Creator. They are here by choice to help you and They do so by loving you like a brother. They serve you all by serving the Plan of the Creator.

You, too, are on your way to mastery and Masterhood. You may do so slowly or more rapidly. But, you may not not go. You may create all manner of experience for yourself along the way. But you did not create yourself. Thus, you too are part of the Plan.

Imagine now that you have this wise older brother who loves you and who has set as His task aiding you in your growth. You don't even have to ask. He is already there, just as I am. We are One. Take comfort in this and let it give you a new view of who you are and why you are here. Let these truths begin to answer the questions of existence and the very meaning of life.

It is a mark of a certain level of maturity that man has begun to earnestly seek after the answers to the great questions. It is also a mark of one of the dynamics of Creation that when you ask, you receive. The response of the Masters to the plight of suffering humanity is required of Them. Man's invocation has a parallel and mandatory response mechanism and it results in an evocation of response from the Masters. It is the law and this They do gladly. This is Their joy for it is Their service. Long have They awaited this opportunity to return to a closer relationship with you. You, They cherish just as you will grow to cherish Them. Responding to the call of mankind, which is now coming from all over this troubled world, is what They have been planning for. They have been waiting for just such opportunity as is presented by the current world situation so that They can again come into closer physical contact with you.

This day do They literally walk among you. This day, right now, They are spread out all over the planet, in all societies and while They work still behind the scenes, They are emerging more and more every day into direct physical contact with you as your growing consciousness will now permit. This service is Their joy. They are grateful for the awakenings of the time for it gives Them the window of opportunity They need to bring Their energy more directly onto the material plane and thus hasten the day of the next great unfolding. This is nigh and They serve its happening to the benefit of all.

You have alluded to the problems of our time and noted the very serious nature of what now faces us. Are You referring to such issues as degradation of the environment, violence, hunger, and homelessness?

Yes.

Masters must be very powerful beings. Is this true?

Yes.

It sounds as though They possess the ability to intervene directly and save us from these problems.

They do.

What are They waiting for? If They love us so, then how can They stand by and not move to fix these things? Given the state of things, we need Them to "come on down" now. Why must They "emerge"? Why can't They just do it?

Among the great gifts and true miracles of Creation is man's free will. It is given under the law. No Master would ever violate this law.

Hierarchy can only work within that law. As I have told you, They are working on your behalf every day. Were They not, things would be grave instead of dire. They do a great deal but always within the law. If a Master were to intervene directly He would take away your choice. This would return you to a state of dependency. To be like your Creator, in whose image you were created, you must have choice. Without choice you may not grow ever more into that image. Among the many characteristics of the Creator, which we have covered here, is your creativity. No choice would mean no creativity.

Masters have latitude to help but must stop short of violating the law. They may give ideas, They may stop certain happenings, They start certain happenings, but They cannot take the wishes of the little ego and make them manifest. Also, while They may mitigate your karma to some degree, They may not eliminate it. This power even They do not have.

So what They do for you is very great. They have been doing it for thousands of years. Now is the time and the window of opportunity for man himself to become a conscious partner with the Masters. Their reappearance among you at this time is to more and more directly help. But They cannot "just do it" for you.

Man is past the childhood dependency stage of development. While the Masters eagerly provide you with great and significant help, it is up to man to take it. To do this you must first recognize the need and then recognize that the help is there. In some ways the recognition of the need remains the greater obstacle still for the great majority of you. Even though recent global events have appeared to galvanize awareness of major issues and some would think spur awakening to ever greater understanding of the deep and serious nature of humanities many and compounding crises, there are many who retreated quickly from the edge of greater awareness. The underpinnings continue to crumble and the basic structures no longer support the system or life. The revelations and pace of global events demonstrate this clearly but the fear of the new and change is strong in man and has engendered a great capacity to believe that the old may yet be restored. There are those who choose even in the face of this overwhelming evidence, still to seek and hear above all else the siren song of the status quo, of the old, of just holding on. Many, out of fear and terror, simply are not able to let go yet, and so above all rationality they continue to choose the insanity of separative thinking. Nowhere is this more evident than in the words of those who trumpet the old theories generated from perceptions of the validity of the insanity. This shortsighted and very dangerous approach is especially true among those who still treasure above all else the economy based on material things expressed through money.

Denial is being used inappropriately to deny that there is anything really wrong or at least that if there is, it is not too serious. This denial has become especially acute in America where it is aided by active efforts to confuse, deflect, deceive, and conceal. This is the great challenge of America's time and role as she is blessed with the very power to lead her brother nations at a time of great crisis.

Lest we give in to fear, never doubt that love and kindness is at work every moment to ease the strain and avoid the sudden "snapping of the rubber band" to use your analogy. Many there are who are ready for this turning in thought. Many there are who have made the turn and realize that you must embrace the new and allow the old to pass away. This is the point to which the race has now come. It is a balance and there is shifting in the direction of right relationship and wholeness. However, much work remains.

To your question then of why the Masters do not just step out and fix it, there are many things They must consider as They too are bound by the law. By emerging into your consciousness the Masters can get your attention without violating your free will. They have chosen this way in order to gradually move to gain your awareness. This allows you to become aware of Them in a way that will make it easier in the long run and protect the right of any to refuse to accept the reality of the existence of Masters. This is yours to decide.

So, to the question of what are They waiting for, They are not waiting in the sense that They do nothing or artificially await some appointed hour. They have been working behind the scenes of human evolution for many thousands of years. There was a time when They were able to work more openly with man. That time has come again.

How do They go about this work?

The Masters are in charge of the Plan on Earth. The part of the Plan seen by Them is much more vast than that which is seen by lesser evolved humanity. They are the custodians of the part of the Plan which applies to man's immediate evolution. They guide its implementation. Masters have an active role in the evolution of the Plan. They take the part of the Plan known to Them and actually develop the implementation details—then put those into effect. It is then determined how well the implementation is going and adjustments are made or courses of action abandoned as the Masters see the need.

Toward this end, They meet regularly to assess progress and to incorporate new visions. Every 25 years They have a major conference to set the general outline of the work for the next 25 years. In this way, They stay focused on the greater unfoldment as They manage the steps necessary to its working out on the Earth.

Masters too are evolving. Their evolution is just as much a part of the Plan as your own. By Their service Masters are growing in Their own wisdom and capacity to see ever greater parts of the Plan and to render that vision into practical manifestation.

At the head of Earth's group of Masters is the great Lord, the One They all look to for wise counsel and loving leadership. He in turn consults Them on Their various aspects of the operation and draws upon the wisdom of the group for His direction. He also receives support and guidance from Those with greater vision and more highly evolved capacities than His own. While it may be difficult for you to imagine Beings more highly evolved than Masters, there are. These Beings are Themselves lesser to greater Ones than They. The aggregation of this great chain of Being is one way to think of God.

Masters then represent your connection to the higher and are working to bring about a greater understanding of the Universe and its working out to mankind. Indeed it will be this knowledge interpreted through Their wisdom which will inform and initialize the next great unfoldment. It is underway now and has been for some time. It cannot be stopped. However, once the significance of this is understood by man, he will want to embrace it. He will rush to embrace it for not only is it his salvation, it will be his joy, his bliss, and his new life.

Mankind stands on the very threshold of awareness of how things actually work and of becoming a conscious partner in its workings. Mankind stands on the threshold of knowing the Creator in ways that man has never been able to before. This knowing will mean a giant step forward in your evolution. This step will be taken with the aid of the Masters and will take you into much closer contact with Them. Of this They are acutely aware and for Them the time immediately ahead is one of heightened alertness and concentration as They bring all of Their efforts to bear on guiding this movement and time of great transition.

As noted, at the head of Earth's group of Masters is the great Lord. He is the leader of the Hierarchy of Masters and has earned this place by virtue of His demonstrated light and love and power. It is He who embodies the love energy. He does not just represent or teach the love of Christ, He is that love energy and thus is properly called the Christ. He along with His great brother, The Buddha, contact directly the energy coming from higher levels and bring it down and render it to you and the other kingdoms of Earth. This is what Hierarchy does and at its head is The Christ.

His very presence brings joy. He is working to bring that joy to the world. He loves each of you, His younger brothers, with the love and affection of an elder brother who is privileged to watch over and guide younger siblings.

He has told you that you, too, will do as He has done ". . . and greater works . . ."[11] This reference was to the evolution of all. You, too, will one day be a Master. All humans are moving thus to become Masters. In so doing you will do greater than He had done at the time He made that statement. You will also, one day, know, too, the love of Christ as One with it.

Am I blocking some of this?

Yes.

You are thinking this is too radical and people will not be accepting of it. You miss the point that this is not about what people will or will not accept relative to your own little self as messenger, but is about giving them choices of new information from which to select. Also, you have been told that many, many there are who are waiting for this and in need of this. The great cry from mankind is for more and more of the higher knowledge and wisdom as mankind is coming to see that what is currently known is not working. It is your fear of offending them. This is incorrect perception. Giving choices from a position of love may give offense to the little ego but is liberation to the higher-self. Take the gloves off and let it flow.

A Master, including the Master of the Masters, is simply more highly evolved than you are. He is not, however, separated from you by this evolution so that He is to be viewed with awe. He is to be treated with the respect that a younger person should show to a loving elder. You reserve awe for the One who created you lest your awe become a block between you and the Master and all of your elder brothers of the Hierarchy. Remember, They are reaching out to you all the time. They are seeking contact with you as you are awakening to the need and possibility of this contact.

How do They contact us?

In many ways including impressions in dreams and the placement of specific and tailored to you individually, powerful symbols as you go through your day. They also will take the guise of a person whom you will trust and may actually have conversation with you.

For some more advanced, They may use a method of contact known as overshadowing. This involves a sharing of the Masters higher consciousness with that of a willing disciple. Willing is the operative word here for no Master would ever attempt such without the full agreement and continued acceptance of the disciple. Overshadowing is done at times to give the Master a more direct vehicle to the lower material plane and involves putting His great energy down for a purpose. This purpose is always that of the greater good. When overshadowing is done, the one who consents to be used so is giving a great gift and also receives a great gift. He is not displaced but more dramatically enhanced. His life and consciousness go on and he is worked through as a vehicle not put aside. He can stop the happening at any time just by saying no and the Master will instantly withdraw his focus. However, this would not be happening in the first place if the invitation to work in this way had not at some level gone out. It was in this way that the Great Lord overshadowed his disciple, Jesus, in Palestine 2000 years ago.

Tell me again how You, the Holy Spirit, work in this line of communication?

About the Holy Spirit—one way of thinking of the Holy Spirit is that It is the Spiritual energy of God that permeates the Universe. This energy is in communion with the Soul.

Tell me more of the nature of the Soul and its working.

The Soul is the individual spark of God in you and all of your brothers. It is within the energy field of your Soul that you live and move and have your being. The Soul is, in turn, a differentiated part of a greater being within whose energy field it does live and move and have its being.

The Soul is on a journey. The personality is an evolving awareness into which the Soul has actually put a spark of its own consciousness so as to learn the lessons of the material plane. This spark has accepted, for a while, that the little personality is the reality. It is this acceptance of an unreal situation that is the basis for the assertion that all is illusion. As the Soul grows in its understanding of the energy of matter and its manifestation on the material plane it gradually comes to understand that the little ego is but a thought projection and begins to assume a larger and larger role in the life of the ego until it, the Soul, comes into its own and, with understanding, overshadows the ego. It is the coming to its senses and gradually recognizing the reality of the higher knowing and its oneness with it, that is the Soul's journey through matter back to its origin. Upon this awakening, you/it/Soul remember who and what you are.

It is into Soul awareness that you must grow. Aware and volitional contact with your Soul is the immediate goal of most humans for only a relative few are there now, though many are at the gate. Indeed it is to assist them that this narrative and many others are being given. This contact marks a plateau in the evolutionary journey and is a turning point.

This is a time of push-pull, and go-stop-go as the new is sensed and moved toward then retreated from. The little ego uses every lure and fear to keep the focus on and continued acceptance of the illusion. The battle is joined. It is the battle of the emerging aspirant and it can go on for several lifetimes until that life comes when it is an understood and increasingly a conscious process. When this happens the turning point is reached where the consciousness of the lower self begins to understand and to actively participate in the awakening. Again, tentative at first, with many retreats and returns to the order of the little ego, to the darkness, but it proceeds. There can be great fear of the light of the Soul and running from its safety.

Remember that there is only One thing. All is connected. So the Soul has the capacity to link with other Spiritual energy such as the Holy Spirit and the energy of the Masters. When a Master contacts you it is first through your Soul, then down to the little personality level.

Soul contact is typically arrived at only after a long period of trial and error in which one progressively tries all the ways of the lower and finds them wanting. The individual brother has come to a place where he can finally say, "There must be a better way." This period is characterized by a growing restlessness with the ways of the lower world. Things that once were engaging and satisfying are no longer so and a searching for the better way, either consciously or not, is going on. Often a series of crises has come with a resulting bewilderment, failure of customary coping techniques and a temporary loss of knowing what to and where to turn. Chaos and a resulting mental anguish can be associated with this phase of development causing many to refer to it as the dark night of the Soul.

Up to this point the individual personality has not been aware of the Soul. The attention has been fixed on the phantasmagoria of the lower world with all of its glamours and desire, and the little ego/personality has been firmly in charge. This new stage is characterized by more and more inclusiveness in one's thinking about their brothers. The problems of suffering humanity become of concern as the sense of separateness begins to give way to the awareness of the unity of all things and a desire to embrace that unity. It is here that the Soul, which has been patiently watching, can exert more and more direct influence over its vehicle: the bodies of the incarnated individual and personality. This process results in the Soul gripping its vehicle and the next level of Spiritual development can begin.

The next phase is one in which the individual begins to consciously participate in their own evolution. You develop the insight and wisdom that comes with contact with higher levels of consciousness. You start to seek out the higher and to understand that with the privilege comes the responsibility to be a conscious and proactive partner in the process. The true meaning of "Knock and you may enter." is learned.

PART NINE

MEDITATE, STUDY, SERVE

What does one do to consciously participate? How does one help oneself to grow?

> The wisdom teaches that three activities are requisite to Spiritual growth. They are meditation, study and service.
>
> The greatest of these is service. By starting with the nearest brother and taking his need as the measure of your response, you begin to break the old patterns of the separated self. Service puts you into a new perspective as you cannot help but see your brother in new ways. In this sense your brother is your teacher and perfect Spiritual partner for he brings the lesson you are in need of. His very presence allows you the opportunity for the growth that you seek. His need is the match for your own. He is your gift from God as you are his.
>
> True service, entered into from the heart, and with no motive but that to serve, not only allows you to embrace the unity of all things; it requires you to do so. It is one of the strongest opponents

of the little ego. True service requires a shift in consciousness to higher levels and away from the focus on the indulgings of the lower. In this sense, true service gets you out of yourself.

True service is ever a joy for it puts you into touch with and synch with the unfolding of The Plan of God. When you serve freely and from a point of love, you are giving in the deepest of ways. It is truly more blessed to give than to receive and service is the perfect and most blessed example of this law for through service you put the love energy of God into the world and set it into motion where it goes on to touch and serve again and again as those you serve find, in their own way, the capacity to serve. The love energy released in service goes to all and is returned to you. This is the law.

Service is the highest calling and can be done by all. There is no one who is not every day brought into opportunity after opportunity to serve. Also, there is not order in the value of service just as there is not order in miracles. Each act of service is a rendering of your natural ability to express God on the material plane and God is an absolute, thus any act expressive of Him is of equal Godliness and, in the case of the shape your world is in, is of equally awesome significance. To serve is to see, acknowledge, become and be One with all; One with God.

Service to the greater good cannot help but also serve you. It is a win-win of such magnitude that it will solve every problem on this Earth. The Masters are returning to the material plane to teach this very lesson and to hasten the day when all look to themselves to serve. When this day comes and come it must and come it will, your world will be saved, for you will have saved it.

Remember that the One great consciousness is unfolding all the time and that it is the very thought of the Creator. Thus serving this unfolding is service to the Plan and is service to God. It is modeled by the Masters. As They serve The Plan of God, so may you. As above, so below.

Study is another of the three ways to grow Spiritually. To study you must only begin to be aware and to listen. There are hundreds of ways that God speaks to you and each contains guidance on where to go to seek more of the information thus derived. Study means to acquire information, which can then be combined into knowledge and acted upon from higher levels through meditation and intuition, which aids the transition of knowledge into wisdom. This should be done in the form which best suits the individual, starting first with the most immediate environment. It is already whispering in your ear and at your fingertips that you find the voice of God. Let your study start there. In every conversation, piece of music, movie, observation, encounter, song, book, television program, web page, and any other source of contact with the world is the opportunity to see the Plan and read the thoughts of the Creator. He put them there for you. You must study these things. You must become a student of these things.

Retrain your mind to be alert for and to actually look for the higher message and the higher wisdom that is all around you. Seek it. Ask for your Soul to help you to see it. One good way to start is to begin to note the number of coincidence encountered. There are no accidents. There are no coincidences. Coincidence is but the unity of all things showing up in your consciousness. Coincidence, if only for a moment, pierces the illusion of separateness. The little ego writes these moments of knowing off; just coincidence. Study to see them as what they are, the voice of God speaking directly to you. After all, it was your coincidence. Wasn't it? It was put into your path so as to get your attention by providing you not only evidence of the unity of all things but an actual point of contact, a point of awareness, a point of re-membering with that unity.

As your understanding grows, you will naturally seek out more focused sources of the wisdom of God. There is more material available than has been opened. Over the last 200 years, man has responded to the part of the Plan calling for greater and more universal education. More people are thus prepared with the needed abilities at a time when the Masters have released the information that Spiritual growth comes through the three requisite activities, one of which is study.

Read the books. Go to presentations. Visit the study groups. View the videos. Attend the lectures. Visit the web sites. And share your new-found information and your newly-focused questions with any who are willing. This, too, is study.

As your wisdom grows, you will naturally sort for what is meaningful to you. It will be consistent with what you need for your path now. Do not judge that for others. They, too, are learning and their path may be informed differently than your own but remember that all paths lead to God. Where you can, honor that which may not be for you and bless your brother on his path. This does not mean, however, that you blindly accept all as coming from a position of right-mindedness. Indeed this is one of the lessons of the study. And when you find a brother or a body of information that has not come from right-mindedness, heal them with love and thus perform the miracle. Do not judge. For this your study has not yet prepared you.

To assist those who may be asking for suggestions on study, you are to include in this when released, a list of some of the sources you have found of value.

The third activity requisite to Spiritual growth is meditation. The point of meditation is Soul contact. Soul contact accelerates your evolution. It renders you wiser as the information coming to you via Soul contact is of a higher nature, quality and vibration. The Soul is patient with you for life after life as you perfect your lower personality to the point that it can be used by your Soul, your higher-self, your first master, to aid the unfolding of the Plan on Earth. Thus, a life comes in which your Soul leads you into closer contact with itself and some form of meditation appears to you and appeals to you. It matters not the form for meditation is as varied as there are seekers after the truth. However, over man's long history, some have evolved as good standard practices. These include the currently popular forms and, like any activity or information toward growth, should be experimented with, embraced and discarded as they prove useful or not.

The goal of meditation is to let you gain and stay in the light of your Soul for progressively longer and longer periods. When there, you are connected and aware. As the practice renders results, you find it easier to do this until a point is reached when it is unnatural to not be so connected. When that time comes, you are ready for the higher work and can be trusted by Hierarchy with parts of the Plan.

Being so able to work with the Plan and to carry out your part is not always a conscious act at the personality level. Many there are who are working under the impress of their Soul who are not yet in possession of the knowledge of the Soul and the relationship of their lower self to their higher self. They include many among you who are doing good and higher work. However, their evolution like all others is toward a conscious awareness of the reality of the Soul and overt contact with their Soul. Many of these people are meditating in some fashion and have been for years in this life and in many previous lives. However, for them their service is great and is the door of their growth into Soul awareness.

It is expected that the release of the information about the existence of Hierarchy and the Soul connection will inform this process further and make this awareness come about sooner. Those who actively engage in meditation, study and service will hasten this day for themselves and their brothers.

If one is thinking about trying meditation, how do they get started?

> Begin by beginning. Go to a quiet place, get physically comfortable, take several slow deep breaths, close your eyes, and acknowledge the existence of your Soul. Then ask for help and guidance. It will come in some form or other. It may not be perceived at that exact moment. It may be seen later in the day in the form of a coincidence or moment of synchronicity.
>
> A good time is early in the day, preferably just after arising. However, there is not a time when overt efforts at Soul connection are not appropriate. Indeed, as you have been told here, the goal will be that of being in contact all the time. This usually requires a period of practice.
>
> If a person is interested in meditation, it is because their Soul has begun to move them in this direction and they will find many references in sources all around them as well as groups which stand ready to help persons interested in meditation. A caveat is needed here. All who are becoming conscious of the path and their way upon it must determine for themselves the steps. They must reserve ever the final determination of what is good practice for them. This should be so of all forms of meditation, study and service. Material presented for study should not be accepted uncritically, but should be tried and subjected to evaluation by the individual. So should meditation practices and service opportunities. The Ageless Wisdom is clear on this point; blind following of any set of precepts is not the way of growth.

To blindly follow is the way of the herd. As noted, man must first learn to come out of the herd and stand as a developed personality. An intelligently critical, not cynical, view of presented opportunities for Spiritual growth is a mark of the unfolding of the process. Then upon acceptance of steps on the path seen to be of value, he can move ever steadily to the point of joining the group. This is the point of the integrated personality joining volitionally with the Soul on its way to becoming one with the Soul.

This discrimination is important to growth also in order that you be ready to discard previously useful practices for newer ones and not cling slavishly to a practice in any of the three activities of growth that has outlived its usefulness for you. Remember you are evolving as an individual in the infinite continuum of consciousness, which is differentiated into distinct points of awareness. Thus, mankind, too, is evolving as a race. This evolution requires that each person come to the point of self-awareness and gain the capacity of independent thought. It is only from this point of having developed fully the separated ego that one can go on to intelligent Soul contact. Otherwise, one remains at an earlier stage such as "he knoweth not that he knoweth not" or at the stage of blind devotion.

Thus, it is understood that there are those further along than others. It is the privilege of those further along to reach out to their brothers who may be behind and, without judgment, and with no sense of superiority or patronization, to serve them. This is, of course, exactly what the Masters are doing for you younger brothers still behind Them on the path. And as the Masters guard your free will so must you guard the free will of your brothers.

May I ask about the dream in which I saw myself stepping down from a table or platform with the help of the person who was wearing the headset?

The dream was from your Soul level not just of the lower vehicle, or body dream variety. You are getting to the point that you can recognize the difference. I speak to you in many voices; this is one of them. Dreams give the opportunity for you to experience the language of the Soul, which is holistic and symbolic. When you get a Soul language message, it is complete. It is at once knowable and known and it comes with all interpretations furnished. In the dream state it is much more clear. As it is brought down to the level of your waking consciousness, its wholeness is often lost and thus interpretation is sought. This inability of the lower mind to hold or fully remember the dream and its unified message will be overcome as you grow in awareness and practice your connectedness. It occurs because the lower self is so ready to accept its centrality and ego focus that it does not yet grasp, it literally does not see, all of the dream.

We need to do more on dreams later.

Some of the stuff You have given me is personal. Is it intended for inclusion in what will eventually be shared?

You are correct that some of this is sufficiently personal that it need not go into the final draft which you will share with others.

Did I just hear the word publish?

Yes, publish is the word.

This particular dream was given to show you that you have made progress and that another step is needed. You were told that you are very close. The image of your needing to step down from your unstable place of isolation is clear to you. It is the place of the little ego. You saw that it required a conscious effort on your part; but that it was not as large a step as it appeared and that when you asked for help to steady the platform so that you could step off of it, that help was readily given.

What step? When?

It will come when you want it. Thus, it is truly said that God does not give you anything that you can't handle. Ask only that it be seen and responded to as the blessing that it is. It will be sweet in its coming. It will be a positioning for the joy that is your birthright.

Why are we referring to Masters always using the masculine pronoun?

Masters are completely balanced in this regard. It is one of the reasons why They are so potent. They have the energy of the male and female interacting in proportion within Them and call upon both and blend them in such a way that each energy type enhances and magnifies the other. It is this balance which renders the issue, the separateness of gender, irrelevant at Their level. Gender separateness with its accompanying specialness is of the little ego.

Masters can appear in either form as need and a particular situation dictates. Most of the Masters, who are emerging now, will take male bodies. This will continue for some time after which others will start to use female bodies. This is because of the nature of the prevailing energy. The prevailing energy is now that of the male. The pendulum has swung far to that of the male energy. Balance is lacking. Indeed it is this lack of balance that has caused so much of the difficulty of your time and which threatens your world.

Because of the nature of the prevailing energy, it requires less energy on the part of the Master to use a male body. As a consequence of the domination of the male energy at this time, males in leadership and public positions are still more accepted than females. While this point is of no consequence to Masters, it is significant to Their being accepted more quickly at this time. Both of these points are important to the Masters relative to Their use of energy. Masters use only the minimum amount of energy needed to accomplish any given task and waste not any energy. Theirs is a task so vast in scope that conservation of energy and its use in right proportion is critical. Indeed, one of the indicators of Masterhood is the demonstration of how to utilize energy efficiently. A Master knows that all is energy and demonstrates the ability to use that energy wisely on all planes.

Neither type of energy is superior to the other. To think this is to indulge the illusion of separateness. It is the disproportion of their expression that is the problem. Masters have evolved beyond this. They are examples of the unity of those energies and demonstrate for you that when seen as mutually supportive, when used in proper combination and juxtaposition, the female and male energy are infinitely more effective than either can be when not supported by the other.

Masterhood is attained through the life experience just as you are experiencing now. Thus, Masters have had many, many lives in each gender and gone through the battle of separation until They were sufficiently experienced to have learned the lessons of unity. This you and all of your brothers and sisters will do.

There is another reason also for the use of the male pronoun and that is to do with the type of influence that the male energy and the female energy exert. The female energy is about intelligence and intuition. The male is about movement and direction. On the material plane it is the male energy that drives the process of constant change. It is on this plane that the Masters direct most of Their efforts at this time to influence the male energy, no matter whether it is manifesting in a male or female body for it is in both and all. They are directing Their efforts toward positive and healing influence and away from negative or wrong relationship directions. Thus, much of the energy in Their own efforts is directed at the energy that will produce the changes, the male energy, so the preponderance of the male pronoun at this time.

How do we know that meditation is getting through? And, while we are at it, what is the difference between meditation and prayer?

> Prayer is focused meditation. Prayer typically involves the asking for a specific outcome or thing. However, the act of seeking higher guidance, of invoking the help of God, is an act of communion with God and as such is a meditation. The term meditation is used more broadly to indicate a more comprehensive and sustained level of that communion. Do not get hung up on the titles lest you engage the duality of the lower. Call it what you wish.

> A maxim of the Ageless Wisdom is that all is energy and that there is nothing but energy. In the entire manifested and unmanifested Universe there is nothing but energy. Thought is energy. To think is to direct energy. To consciously seek to hear or otherwise accept communication from higher sources is to be open to receiving energy, in this case, Spiritual energy. In the ultimate reality All is this Spiritual energy as there is nothing but God.

> You know that meditation is getting through because there is feedback. The material world is full of feedback on the presence and specific messaging of the Spiritual energy. There is a virtual chorus of ways and communications from God. It is there all the time because the Creator placed it there in the Plan and signals to you at every moment from every venue. You must but listen, see, touch, smell, and taste it.

If you are in need of a demonstration, go to any physical plane event or place at which you feel, even remotely, a sense of awe and connectedness to something greater. For you it is the night sky. There is your proof. There is your doorway. There is your Creator. There is your path and promise and way home.

This is a fundamental construct and ongoing process in The Plan of God. It is there to be the precise mechanism that it is, in order to answer the very question you have asked. It is so basic to the Plan that it is under law and like all the laws of God, it has many corollaries.

One such corollary is the law of invocation. This law requires that those of higher evolution must respond to those of lower when they seek contact. It is built into the very fabric of the Universe. The law does not require that this response be what is actually being asked for, a new bicycle for example. It requires that, when contact in any form is sought, that it be responded to with love. It is required by that love then that what is needed most by the person seeking contact and what will serve the highest and greatest good be what is given. While occasionally this may be expressed as an actual new bicycle, it is always for the higher and greater good of the individual and the group.

So when mankind, either as an individual or as a group, meditates and prays, it evokes a response from the Masters. It is the law and it is the joy of the Masters to see and hear this invocation from you. It is your right to expect a response evoked from Them. Look and listen for it.

Once experienced from the level of the senses, you can grow into the level of more direct and conscious awareness and move on to higher levels of knowing and remembering. Such is the progression into higher consciousness. Ultimately, the journey into higher consciousness renders both prayer and meditation, as you now know them, unnecessary as they are replaced with a level of constant communion within which you are no longer aware of God as something that you pray to, but the One that you are. When you set out to pray and meditate, when you say, okay I am now going to pray and meditate, you conceptualize God as separate from you. However, these are necessary steps on the path from that separation to unity. It is the difference between perceiving and knowing.

PART TEN

THE LAW OF INVOCATION

Good morning. It has been a week of disappointment in terms of my time to get to this work. I ask for help here to allow me to get on this work with greater frequency in the future.

You are the one who must make these decisions as to how and when to be available. I am always here and as has been noted before do actually miss you when you are not connected. Your practice will bring a time when you will not lose the awareness of the connection. Joining Me as you are now is one way of reinforcing and moving toward that point of constant awareness. There are many other ways and they come to you all the time.

Yes, you are physically much better and, yes, you were able to connect better during the time of your recent episode of stress. This is because the stress and resulting symptoms motivated you to look for answers and you turned to connectedness in search of them. This is good and should show you validation of your growth.

Child of God, you are at the door of the temple. Knock and you shall enter. It is up to you as to how long you will allow yourself to remain outside.

So the law says that when man asks for, calls for, or invokes help or contact from higher sources that those higher sources must respond. That is, a response is automatically evoked from higher sources.

This is true. It is one of the fundamentals of the Creator. Its corollary is that the evoked response is the joy of the one who is responding. It is a service and true service is ever a joy. Thus, the circle is complete. The one in need gets help and the giver is provided an opportunity to serve. This model holds true between humanity and the Masters as well as among you and your brothers. As above, so below.

May I just recap here please? Prayer is a direct asking while meditation is an effort at the more prolonged contact that You say will result in awareness. Both are efforts at communion. This effort or invocation automatically calls down a response or evokes a response and this is the law.

By George, I think you got it!
This process is so important to the immediate time that the Masters have given a special invocation or prayer for use at this time. It is patterned as close as language and circumstances will allow after an ancient mantrum of great power and can be given out to all mankind only now because of the progress that the race has made toward being able to handle, with some sense of love and

responsibility, such power to invoke the attention of the Masters.

It is called *The Great Invocation* and is used on behalf of all humanity by the Christ Himself every day. All who wish to serve the good in this time are urged to say it every day. It is compatible with all other forms and words of loving prayer and meditation and because it comes from the level of the Masters, it is a perfect fit for the needs of the time and anyone's readiness to serve. When said with focused attention of love and service, it is a powerful force for the good of all and gives the Masters a very clear call that evokes from Them a focused response. It expedites the downflow of Spiritual energy. It is pure service. It is a win/win.

It is for all humanity and belongs to no separate group.

EXERCISE 3

THE GREAT INVOCATION

It is recommended that, at first, you go to a place of solitude and after a few moments of quieting your body, your emotions, and then your mind that you say the Invocation, out loud if possible. Saying this Invocation out loud may not always be possible. When this is so, say it inwardly and remember it is a blessing for yourself and all others even if you are in a room full of your brothers and sisters. It is recommended that you do this every day. It is a good way to begin a daily practice of meditation. It is also recommended that you use it at any other time when you want to reconnect or to strengthen your connectedness.

Begin with the title.

THE GREAT INVOCATION

From the point of light within the mind of God let
light stream forth into the minds of men. Let light
descend on Earth.
From the point of love within the heart of God let
love stream forth into the hearts of men. May Christ
return to Earth.
From the Center where the will of God is known let
purpose guide the little wills of men, the purpose
which the Masters know and serve.
From the center which we call the race of men, let
the Plan of love and light work out and may it seal
the door where evil dwells.
Let light and love and power restore the
Plan on Earth.

Are there other recommended practices of prayer and meditation?

> Funny you should ask. There are many forms and each will find one that is a starting place given their own point of development and readiness.
>
> Yes, there is another that should be mentioned here. It is called Transmission Meditation and is a powerful yet simple form of meditation that is at the same time a great service. You might call it a twofer as it combines two of the three practices requisite to Spiritual growth: meditation and service.
>
> Transmission Meditation is a practice given by the Masters to all. It, like *The Great Invocation*, belongs to no special group and is compatible with all other forms of right-minded prayer and meditation. As its name implies, it is a form of transmitting. In this case, it is a way of transmitting the energy used by the Masters. When you are doing this practice you are engaged directly in helping Them to move energy from higher levels down to the material plane. Thus, you meditate and serve at the same time. It may be done individually but is best done in groups if possible. There are hundreds of such groups around the world today. The technique is simple and can be learned in just a few minutes. Those who find a responsive chord here are encouraged to learn more about this practice and to find a group near them within which to do this vital service or to start such a group.

What responses do we get from the Masters? If we ask for bicycles but need something else, what is the else that we get?

> The Masters are your elder brothers and have been behind the scenes of human evolution for thousands and thousands of years. It is They who have guided the implementation of the Plan on Earth. It is this for which They are responsible and it is Their service and joy.
>
> They see the suffering caused by separation and are moving always to comfort, help, reduce, and where you, mankind, are now actively cooperating with Them, to heal the separation and bring you home to God. They have walked the path that you now trod. They are holding out the hand of help to you. They speak for you at higher levels. They connect you to the greater cosmos. It is They who are the vehicles for the higher energy to flow to you.
>
> Masters are the link in the great chain of being between where you are and where you are going. They are the proof of the Plan's working out and of your part in it. They hold wide the door and actively help you to and through it. They are the example of where your progress through evolution will take you. Remember, all life on Earth is evolving through the human stage to Masterhood. All will be Masters. Thus, it was truly said by the Christ through His disciple in Palestine ". . . I am the way, the truth, and the life: no man cometh unto the Father, but by me."[12]

So the first thing that They do is to take the Plan of the Creator as They are given it, and devise strategies and plans of Their own of how to make it manifest within the sphere of Earth. One such strategy is that of Their now moving to emerge into your consciousness and to once again enter the physical world more directly with you. This is a great happening and is in part Their response to man's cries for help, man's invokings, which have become so great because so many are suffering unbearably.

Their strategies and plans include all manner of activity up to the limits of the law. Masters are at the scene of disasters great and small to help remove the fear. In this way They provide comfort and ease the transition for those whose physical life ends in this way.

They are present in the circles of world leadership where They attempt to inspire world leaders with thoughts of love and the truth that all men are brothers, unified under one Creator. In this regard They "impress" those leaders with concepts, ideas, thoughts, and inspirations. However, as always, one is free to pursue or reject any impression.

Masters are present in the worlds of science, economics, medicine, education, politics, religion, business, and all other areas where man has organized his thought and activity. Working through advanced disciples in all fields, They are shaping the future by encouraging mankind to wake up and become constructive, responsible, active partners in mankind's own evolution. Mankind has reached a critical stage of development where it is an active partner in its own evolution. However, all too often you, mankind, are an unconscious, destructive partner. This has reached the point of crisis and threat to the continuation of the race. This energy of crisis has brought about the great outcry or invoking of millions and is giving the Masters the way to move, to evoke a response by moving closer to you and to working directly with you. That is what Their reappearance, Their emergence, at this time, is all about.

To the extent that They may do so, within the law, They are mitigating the karma of your self-destruction. They are, for example, helping to dampen the effects of pollution including nuclear. This is buying you time to awaken further to the brotherhood of all mankind and to respond to this threat. However, They can only do so much, for ultimately man is responsible to change himself and his ways. They stand ready with wisdom, insight, and technical help but man must now see the need to do this of his own hand. This is the group that man must now join: Out of the herd and into the group.

They are also releasing the seed thoughts of the new technologies, those which can be safely so released. They will not yet put into your hands many advances that will, when developed, give you powerful tools to control energy. This is because these tools may also be powerfully abused if not used with love and in service to the greater good.

But, more than anything else, the Masters are teachers. Indeed, the One who now embodies the Christ energy, who in effect holds the office of

Christ for this time, the Great Lord and Master of the Masters, says of Himself that He is the world teacher and prefers to be known in this way. It is this teaching role that the Masters cherish and seek to place most of their energy, for it is there that They can be of the most help. In order to do this They are positioning Themselves to come into direct and more immediate physical proximity with you.

A friend and member of the meditation group told us of an impression she had during the meditation period. It was a very clear and lovely vision of human unity of thought and purpose. When she told us about it I experienced an immediate sense of knowing and acceptance of what she said. It was a reaction in me at several levels including mind, heart and gut. There was a trueness and sweetness about the content. It was for the group but each of us also got something individually from it. May I know more?

It was a gift from the Master to give you all encouragement, for your work is important. It touched each of you at your point of most focus at that time. As you noted then it was the perfect gift as it evoked a corresponding gift. It was your healing session for the night.

As for you, it but restated and validated what you have heard here—that the promised more, much more, is to and will come and that you should lighten your heart. Lightening your heart will help others to do so. It will position you better to receive the gifts that are rightfully yours. Lightening your heart will literally make it easier for you to share and give and thus to receive.

You have many times told me to knock. You have told me ". . . you are at the door of the temple. Knock and you shall enter." What door? How do I knock on it?

> The door to the next level: the door to your unfolding consciousness; the door to which you are so close; the door to your birthright of joy; the door to the temple; the door to better understanding; the door to knowing; the door to Me and your Master; and the door to greater connectedness and your next stage of the work.

> You knock by connecting and reconnecting and reconnecting again until it becomes automatic and instinctual. You knock by learning that "action is the key to your life's door." You knock by asking. You knock by seeing yourself knocking, by reframing your view of the Universe to that of a disciple. You knock by storming the gate that separates you from your brother. You knock by holding his hand to help him pass through the gate of fear into the light with you.

> You knock for many others who even now look to you and need you to shelter them and show them the way.

What do I do about the brother at work who has so clearly done something unacceptable at the personality level? I am being directed by another brother to treat him in a way that does not appear right. It appears to me that I am being directed to attack when persuasion and kindness are my preferences.

> There are old debts here. Do not see it from the level of the personality. Just as you are learning to

separate the personality from the actions of others, learn to see here too that there is a bigger picture and that good will come of it. Good will come of all as all things work together for the greater good.

Okay, but I am being called upon to be the instrument of unkindness.

Detachment is your key. Do what you are directed to do with love and detachment. You had many lessons yesterday. See them in perspective. You had proof of those who look to you for help. You had the opportunity to show and share your wisdom. It is all part of the bigger Plan. This troubles you because you have not let go of your own personality control and judgment. It is a burden. Put it down. It will lighten your heart.

I was told to "Put the fear in him." Help me with this language and its intent.

This is personality hyperbole and comes from the fear of the brother who said it. Your buying into it does not help to heal the fear behind this behavior.

What of a positive nature can I do for both of these brothers in order to serve best?

You know that the tyrant is that of the little ego. You do not serve it. Be patient. Be there, present in your own center and act as a balance. Your very presence, when you are centered, is such a force. It is one of the reasons you are where you are. This is the time for you to learn this. This is the time for you to develop your detachment and ability to influence with love/wisdom. Choose your moments and also balance with the law of occult silence.

Remember what the Master has told you to practice: Honesty of mind, Sincerity of Spirit and Detachment.

Your residue of doubt still plagues you. Let go and let God. Let go and let the Plan work. Have joy.

Thank You. Where do we go from here on the book?

Where would you like to go?

Can You make a suggestion?

Okay. Let us discuss some positive actions that can alleviate the current crisis.

What current crisis? Can we delineate the current crisis first?

The current crisis is that of the failure of the race to recognize its power and responsibility. Misuse of the power in irresponsible ways has brought about a clear danger of destruction of your physical form. Failure of your systems to support your physical life is now foreseeable and imminent. It is also still preventable, though time grows short.

We will not expend precious energy here on the details for there exists already more than sufficient information to convince any thinking person of the truth of this crisis.

Denial ain't just a river in Egypt.

Precisely!

Points of crisis come in the evolution of the race on your planet around every 2000 years. At each point new forms are born as old ones are swept away. Everywhere you look this is happening before your eyes. Sometimes it is so great in magnitude and so swift in coming that it is hard to grasp and it is more expedient to simply ignore it or to deny it. This particular point of crisis has reached that stage and you are in very real physical danger. It is in response to this danger as well as the opportunity for growth into the new that the Masters are more directly entering your world again.

Personal points of crisis come in each life, analogous to the larger national and, at the present time, planetary point of crisis. At both junctures, personal and group, the crisis carries the destruction of the old forms and also the seeds of renewal and growth. In the case of this transition, including as it does the movement into the new millennium, the crises are overlapping and are greater in magnitude. Thus, it is also a greater potential to propel you far in your growth.

So what do we do?

Remember, all is energy. There is nothing but energy. Perception of lack is just that, perception. Spirit knows no lack. There is no lack, there is, in fact an abundance. The Universe is overflowing with blessings, material and other, placed there by the Creator for you; for all of you. The energy is in motion and brings the abundance to you in cycles as you need it and in the form that you need and at the time that you need it. There is a time to every purpose.

However, when you do not recognize the abundance and are fearful to the point of blunting your natural inclination to share and cooperate, you dam the flow of this holy energy. When you fear that you will be deprived, because you see a brother whom you perceive as deprived, and mistakenly conclude that if his need is met then yours will not be, and you choose to respond not with love and its corollaries of sharing and cooperation to that brother's need but by withholding, then do you not only dam the flow but you damn this flow and the energy stops moving and you stop receiving. In this way you literally stop the flow of abundance to you and your brother.

Thus, as we have noted here before, it is truly more blessed to give than to receive. This is because the act of giving ensures the flow. It primes the pump and starts the pump. In the act of giving is the essence of receiving. It only works this way. It is cause and effect, which is another of God's laws.

It is the difference between perception and knowing.

I grow concerned over my slowed pace in this work. There have been many distractions including physical fatigue, etc.

We would prefer a stronger pace. You must manage these things of the lower as they are illusional but for now real to you.

What help or suggestion do You have for me at this moment?

> This narrative, your learning to connect, your growth in the awareness, and the continuation of the call are all help to you. Your reading of A Course In Miracles is a help. It is especially good at what you need to know now. Thus, it is a "just-in-time" gift.

I dreamed of a book, which appeared to me as a familiar text but also seemed to be clearly different. I recalled being told that I would write a narrative and not to doubt. I thought that this could be what I was seeing and thought that it was different from the work of this journal, at least so far. Can You help me with this?

> There are many works to be done. This is but one of them. Others there are who are also working. Your place in the work will be determined, in part, by what and how and when you do it. It flows together as there is only One work. This is one of the points to be made in this journal, that it is correlative to other and all pieces of the greater work to which many have contributed and are contributing.

So I glimpsed the greater work?

> Symbolically yes, you saw the great book of knowledge. And you understood that you are helping to bring its contents to your brothers who are not yet ready to read it directly. You are sensing, seeing parts which are in your capacity to grasp and are being asked to serve by rendering them into a form which may be reached by brothers who are ready to receive at the level and in the form so connected

by you. Others there are who see more clearly and more largely than your current capacity. From these you, in turn, are being taught. It is to their level or capacity that you are reaching. The chain is unbroken and flows to them in their turn from yet higher levels.

Remember that there is not prestige in level as there is not order in miracles. That is of the ego.

I am chafing at some current situations at work but can't see not being there and doing that work, at least for now.

You have been told that you are in the right place. This is still true. There are lessons for you there and much service to be done. Some have already come to you. This is evidence of the validity of your placement. Others there are who would come but for their fear. Give them and you time to mature.

All will be well.

I suppose I look still for the magic bullet.

Yes, and have it in your hand all along.

But You told me that there is no magic bullet.

This is true.

Help me with this contradiction.

It is not a contradiction. The magic is in transcending the desire for the bullet and knowing that you are it. This is coming to you now. Thus it is in your hand.

Did I just hear that this is enough for this morning?

Yes.

Why?

The pace is sufficient for now. It will change as the energy changes. Go with the flow. Use this time to review, edit, and clean up your text. There is a time to every purpose under heaven.

PART ELEVEN

THOUGHTS ARE TRULY THINGS

More please about sharing and cooperation.

Both are acts of love and are the natural outpouring of your connectedness to your brother and the Universe. At the material level, sharing is the physical acknowledgement of the unity principle and is expressed simply and directly by the giving of material things to meet the needs of your brothers. While this is most typically thought of as basic needs, it is really any need including freedom from want and security from physical harm.

This also includes higher abstract needs such as growth in learning and knowledge to include help on the path of Spiritual growth. Thus, any true need of your brother should be the indicator of what, if you have it, you should share.

Sharing is the hallmark of growth toward higher Spiritual levels as it is a direct expression of the unity principle. As one gains even the most rudimentary of awareness into the unity of all things, it becomes increasingly more and more difficult to see those in need and not desire to do something about it. This is now happening on a larger and larger scale throughout humanity and is evidence of the general level of growth of the race. This is indicative of the level and kind of change in the energy of the very thought processes of mankind at both the individual and group levels.

This capacity to begin to see the need of your brothers and to begin to awaken to the task of doing something about it, through sharing and greater cooperation, is a significant item in the emergence of the Masters. This is because They can respond to this newly awakening energy. It is a field of energy within which They can work. Indeed Their task up to now has been to help you grow to the point of being able to generate this type of energy within some semblance of volition

Mankind has grown to this level so that this type of energy, the energy of the higher unity, can now begin to become manifest. The fact that it is happening, even rudimentarily, is vital to the next step in the human evolution which will permit the Masters to once again walk openly among you. This is happening now.

The Masters have been sharing and cooperating with you, (humanity) to move you to a point where you see and act upon this from your own initiative and center. That process being modeled by the Masters and seen as developing, even rudimentarily, in mankind allows for the next unfolding. This development creates the energy field, the environment, within which the Masters can come more directly to more of you. This allows Them to do more for you at higher levels and reflects directly what you are beginning to do for each other on the material plane.

One of the first things that the Masters will urge you to do is to dramatically expand the sharing and cooperation to include all of your brothers on the planet. This will further strengthen the energy fields of love and will allow for future connections to the Masters and Their work and will thus further reinforce the cycle of growth for all. This is the way growth occurs. It comes out of the previous growth and builds upon it and spirals up, ever upward to higher levels of awareness. The fact that so many are still shackled by the absence of the most basic of the physical requirements of life is a major factor retarding the growth of all. Remember it is a package deal. There is only one Father and you are all coming home.

Sharing is governed by the rule of giving and receiving. That which you truly and with loving intention give away comes back to you. It goes into the flow at the material level but also into the flow of Spiritual energy as the intent to give and returns to you in the exact intent as you expressed it. It will thus meet your need whatever that need may be. Thus, the intent is more important than the actual gift. Hence the widow's mite was a colossal gift not only because of its relative proportion to her material wealth but because of the love energy which motivated the gift and because she had no other motive but to give. It is in this state of consciousness, aware only of the greater unity and the loving desire to contribute to it, that it is truly said what you give you get.

This is an expression of the law of cause and effect and it works 100 percent of the time for 100 percent of mankind. It is truly said that which you sow also shall you reap. The higher expression of the law then has to do with the intention. When you share, the motivation is the key, for that determines what goes into the flow of the higher energy. It is what goes into the flow that returns to you. In this regard you are directing energy with your mind. This is the great capacity that man has evolved into and which now gives you such power to create and destroy. Man must become aware that he has such power and that to continue to abuse it in separative thinking, that is, in placing negative energy into the flow, will continue the cycle of destruction. Man must also know that the opposite is true.

Thoughts are truly things and take on an energy commensurate with the motivation that is behind them. The more highly evolved a person becomes, the more powerful becomes their capacity to create coherent and more powerful forms of thought. These thought-forms continue in an existence of their own. If they are reinforced from the source or from others, they grow. They can be extinguished by opposite thoughts and fear. However, all of you are creating all the time. While most of this thought is still random or so chaotic as to not have any real impact on the happenings of the time, the cumulative effect is still highly potent in returning to you in the flow. This is why so much of what you do every day is within the context of fear because so much of what the race is putting out in thought energy is of a fearful nature. Thus, so much of what you are receiving, getting back, is of a fearful nature which in turn reinforces the nature of what is thought and returned to the flow of energy as negative thought energy of fear. It is a cycle that must be broken. You now have the capacity to do that. With this capacity comes the responsibility to act. By understanding then the law of cause and effect you have accessed one of the Creators most powerful tools and can, if you intend it, quickly move to set your house in order by right motivation in thought. This is what is meant by being right-minded. Right mindedness will lead naturally to right relationship which is characterized by right action of sharing and cooperation.

Thus, man's future is bright, very bright indeed, if you so choose. Or you may continue on the path of not thinking of your brother as yourself, the path of separation and of ego. This path is the path of assured destruction because you intend, will, and guarantee it to be so by the motivation of your thought.

It is not hard to see what the dark future would be like. What will the bright future be like?

The new golden age, more glorious than you can now see, will come. This is the true meaning of the new age. It will be a flowering of all that is good and true and beautiful. Not just an end to hunger and the blasphemies of separation but a coming in of their opposites in fully equal measure. To the extent that there is hunger, exposure, violence, fear, neglect, and the Earth itself in rack and seeming ruin will come the opposite. This is the law of cause and effect. The pendulum will swing not to return to neutral but will go past that and will re-bracket into a new era of not just the end of these terrible things but into and a coming forth of their opposite at a level of intensity equal to the current intensity of negative energy.

This is a critical concept and must be understood for it holds the key to the way out of the current crisis. It is the ideal which awaits only man's right-mindedness to become the real. Man has reason to be hopeful as many there are waking up to the knowledge of the power inherent in the capacity to conceive of another way. By conceiving of it you create it first in thought. Then these thought-forms become manifest on the material plane. This will be one of the greatest accomplishments and giant evolutionary steps of the race. It is precisely this that the Masters are equipped and motivated to help you attain.

However, while you may not now be able to see this bright new future, you can imagine it. This, too, is a vital point for in it is the power to create just as your Creator creates and as you are endowed to do. You create new and alternative thought-forms by the use of the creative imagination. Remember that your thoughts have power because they are real things. Thus, to imagine a bright new future is to contribute to its coming into manifestation on the material plane.

Therefore, imagine and dream large, very large. See a future, near at hand and ready to come to pass, that is the place of light where you are fully in possession of your birthright of joy, where every brother is beaming with the love energy of the Creator. See a place where your cities are clean and shining, where your rivers run crystal to a sea that is not just unpolluted but friendly. See a world where every child comes into a loving place and every adult welcomes that child as his own. Imagine a world where nature and man cooperate in the creation of light, sound, color and warmth which penetrates every darkness and enriches every hour. Create in your mind a world where every day is unlike the one before as the Plan of the Creator unfolds before your delighted senses and where you know of your Oneness with that Plan. Picture, literally see in your mind, a world profoundly at peace, a world where peace is palpable and tasted as a constant background and undertone on the tongue of every living thing. Visualize a whole world, The whole world, sitting down to a feast of new awareness and consciousness of God Himself and anxious only to share it with each other and to relish the giving and receiving of it one to the other. Imagine a Universe where this is the norm, where this is the law, and whereby you, contributing your own necessary creative piece of it to the higher good, ensure its manifestation and continuation.

See this world in terms of the unity of things now seen as separate. See the lion lie down with the lamb. Create in your mind the picture of harmony in all of nature with mankind serving and being served by its lower kingdoms. Visualize the harmony as such that the very elements, now in upheaval, are a sweet symphony with music in the breeze, paintings in the skies, and meaning on every wing. A world where every word is a symphony and every step is a dance.

Picture also the temple, now obscured, standing radiant, glistening in the sun and recognized by every brother and sister as the holy meeting place of all God's family. See it glow with the light of love and see it being maintained by sharing and cooperation.

Utopia?

Yes, and better than any so far grasped by mankind. For this time is at hand. Man has grown to the point that the help of the Masters can come in such quality, abundance and directness as to render these visions but shadows of what will be. This need be no longer the far horizon which beckons to you from some distant someday. It is now and is unfolding as we speak. This is the true meaning of the new age. This is the way of the future and requires only that you choose it to be so.

The Master of the Masters Himself has said that He has seen the heart of man and that you will choose the higher way. The Great Lord has said "All will be well".

What a wonderful vision; makes one want to get on with it.

That is what it is supposed to do. There is no reason to wait one minute longer before embracing this higher and clearly better way. Delay is because of ignorance and fear. The ignorance is being taken care of by the inflow of the knowledge of higher realms and their accessibility. The fear must be taken care of by each person. Fear is of the mind. It is created there and it can be left behind there.

PART TWELVE

FOLLOW YOUR BLISS

Is there an order in the time of my awakening to the call each night to get up and write this journal? Is there a qualitative difference between the first call of about midnight and the next of about 2:30 a.m.?

> Not really, you are called all the time, every minute of every day. It is just easier to hear when the ego sleeps and after the body has had some rest. This is usually in the quiet of the earliest part of the new day. It is then that you can focus more easily on the work without the press of the material world. The goal is to reach the point that the call is easier to respond to than the lower world at any time of day. This will give you the constant connection and awareness that is the natural state.

About being connected, is there a way to know or sense more dramatically the connection? As I remember to connect during the day and use the OM with focus on the ajna center, I do not have a sense of any difference in my mental state.

> That is because there is none.

Then am I connecting when I do that?

> Yes, you are. The sensation of the rush of bliss is
> what you are seeking. As noted earlier, this is not
> happening as it did during an earlier phase of your
> awakening because the connection is becoming
> more routine and natural. However, that is not to
> say that you are routinely connected. Your efforts
> will be needed in the form of practice until you no
> longer have to think to practice but have the intent
> and focus all the time.

Is there feedback that will tell me that I am connected?

> Yes, listen for a sound. You will begin to hear the
> music.

What I often hear now is ringing.

> That is the background. It is the first step in the
> hearing of the celestial music.

So I can do the connection exercise like that of
Transmission Meditation and then listen for the music
to follow at that point?

> Yes.

Thank You. I will try this.

I hear "Go to bed." Is this the lower wanting to return to
the comfort of sleep?

> It is.

As I thought. So where do we go from here?

Where would you like to go?

Higher! To return to the bliss and stay there. I would like to lighten my heart as I have been told. Any suggestions on this?

Just do it!

And to do it?

> It is there in front of you. Continue to take each step and seek the laughter in each step. See the humor and its underlying construct, the joy. Pause for those moments when they come to your attention. Examine them. Learn to note the presence of joy in its infinite qualities and expressions. It is there all of the time. You do now literally have it. It is your birthright and has been given you as part of the deal. It is in the Plan. You have but to grasp it. You do this by looking for it, by knowing that it is there. You do not have to manufacture it but only need to connect to it. What is required is a conscious and constant act of the will until the act is sufficiently accomplished to become automatic.

Dear One. Thank You. I am beginning to grasp some of this at least. It is still hard for me to see where we are going with it. But the idea of a book and the broader sharing of this information is appealing. I am looking forward to the class I will teach on meditation and the working with people on meditation. I would much rather be doing that than other things.

> Follow your bliss. This is the path of least resistance and is where your true self lies. However, you will find that giving up the desire for control and

171

replacing it with the desire for service will eliminate the duality of preferences like the one you just noted, for then you become the path and are not trying to choose a better one.

Take a note pad with you on your trip. We have done work on airplanes and in airports before.

So when we get to the point that You have said will be revealed to me, the point of publish, then what?

Other doors will open and you will be given choices of service.

How are we doing?

The little ego remains strong and grows more confused as you wrest control from it. This is indicative of the point of your development. It is start stop, push pull, go and don't. Thus, you can see that your behavior is markedly different from that of even a few months ago. Your work with this narrative will be such that those at similar stages will relate to it.

Don't doubt, just do. Action is the key to your life's door. Continue to act. Movement in and of itself is valuable. The observation about shuttle diplomacy is correct. Sometimes just the activity of doing generates the environment which promotes progress.

Airborne at this time. We have done some good work in the air.

Yes. There is no place where we may not do more good work.

I don't hear the music yet.

> You will. Just as you asked for many years to hear My voice, when you are ready you will also hear the music. You have heard it before. You have been told to listen to your song celestial and to let it be sung for you. Look for it and expect it. In the looking you create the happening as you anticipate, empower, and connect to what is already there. This is an act of creation.

I feel somehow that questions and answers that are more personal in nature are taking time away from the greater work, the book You have said will come.

> This may be true. Remember that this material is first for you, then others. Only as you grow in this way can you position yourself to share at the level needed. Also, you do not know what the final result will look like and so for now all is potential for inclusion.

You have referenced that it will be for others at some point to read this. How will those whom eventually share in this work know that it is true?

> The acid test, the only test will be whether or not it works for them. There can be no other basis of authenticity, rightness, wrongness, inspiration, or lack thereof for anything found here. The sisters and brothers coming upon this work must decide using all information available to them including intuition.

When the time comes advise them, as you have so often advised those who may have asked about study in the area of their own Spiritual development, that if they have any sense that there may be some truth here for them, they may wish to consider giving it 50 pages or so of their energy in the form of attention to the text. If the content has not spoken to them in some way or rings unclear or untrue for them, then they should put it down and move on. It is not for them at this time.

There are so many themes. The one that continues to come to mind is feedback on how and when I am connected so as to go with the higher in everything.

As noted in <u>A Course In Miracles</u>, ask yourself how do you feel? Be open to an honest assessment of your emotional state and reaction to any situation or at any time. Do a "gut check".

This will tell you much. If you are experiencing negative emotions, if there is pain, guilt, doubt, anxiety, fear, attack, or any other emotion that is not peace, then you have an indicator telling you that you are not connected. It also tells you that you have thought in terms of separation. It tells you that you have judged a brother or yourself and found him or you to be unwhole. That is, separate from the greater unity of all things and thus separated from the Sonship. This judgment causes an unholy condition in your mind. As only the mind can create fear so only the mind can create for itself separation.

Healing of these thoughts will bring a return of the whole and Holiness will again result. This is the miracle. This is the atonement and it lies always within your grasp. As you grasp it and return yourself to the state of Holiness, you contribute greatly to that for your brother. The accomplishment of this feat by any brother energizes the field for all of you and hastens the day and clarifies the way for others who themselves are always only one step from Holiness, one step from God.

EXERCISE 4

A CLEARING EXERCISE FOR WHEN YOU RECOGNIZE THE EMOTIONAL SYMPTOMS OF SEPARATIVE THINKING AND THE UNHOLY STATE OF MIND WHICH HAS RESULTED

Proceed as follows—calm your physical vehicle. Go to a quiet place at first, even if it is the restroom. God is there, too. A quiet place will be important at first. Later, with practice, this exercise will come to you any place.

You calm your physical vehicle by taking several deep breaths, slowly in through your nose and out through your mouth. Close your eyes.

Next, calm your emotional vehicle by bringing all thoughts to a single point of focus. The center between the eyebrows is one such point of focus. Bring all mental focus there. Hold this focus. Return to it several times as needed for in the early stages of learning this technique, your attention may quickly wander.

Next, calm your mental vehicle by asking for communion, guidance, peace, and help. Then declare what you want. Do not indicate that you actually do want it but that you have and are it. For example: "I have the peace of God. I am the peace of God."

Once so centered and connected, go to the thoughts that brought you the pain and heal them with love.

This meditation will serve you well and will increase in its potency with practice. It is better to practice this technique in order to master it during your morning meditation so as to work through it and have it firmly established so as to be ready to call it up at times of need.

This practice may be summed up in the words of the Psalmist, "Be still, and know that I am God." In the act of the stillness comes the knowledge of the One God, the One Unity and your essentialness within It.

When connected, you are in touch with the knowledge of all things. You really do know God. This transcends perception which is of the ego. To perceive something is to see it by definition as separate from yourself. The little ego perceives so that it can confirm its separation and justifies discrimination through judgment of itself and its brothers. To heal this is the atonement, at-one-ment, and it goes beyond perception to knowing.

In the greater scheme you are not going anywhere. You do not have a destination. You are instead there already and must only awaken to your own presence. You awaken into the knowing. You are awakened by the knowing as you become the knowing.

The knowledge is liberating, it is fun. It is your natural state of joy where you do not strive, struggle, compete, or want. It is Being and you already have it. Remember that, to your Holy Spirit, there is no difference between having and being. Also remember that the protection of what you have rests only in its sharing. Thus, it is said of the Holy Spirit that having all, it protects all, by giving it away.

Just be.

I sense a certain repetition.

True. This narrative is designed to touch those at a certain point of readiness as other material is designed for other points. Think of it as segmental marketing. Many themes are initiated and then sequentially developed. Once initiated, they are then broadened and connected to other themes which permit them to become ever more expansive and thus richer and to better inform the consciousness of the aspirant who is drawn to the study at this level.

The process is often referred to as a spiral. As such, you should recognize points on the circular turns as familiar because you have seen them or been there before. However, each time you arrive at a particular point on the circle you are also higher than the last time. In this way you can visualize the evolutionary process as turns of the spiral which allow for your growth and expansion.

Does my growth and expansion allow me to climb the spiral or does its turning allow for my growth?

It is a metaphor. It is the unfolding of the Plan of the Creator that drives all. You are a part of it. It is driven by the same force that causes the flower to grow skyward from the ground and it is the same force that moves the planets, stars and galaxies in their courses. It is the force of Obi-Wan. It is all. It is God.

PART THIRTEEN

KARMA

A dear sister is now very ill.

> She has come to a major point of growth and can
> decide many things for this life as well as prepare
> many things for the next life.

How may I help?

> You may help by your healing work. Send her
> also books and when appropriate, parts from this
> narrative. <u>A Course In Miracles</u> would be good, but
> not yet. She loves you and trusts you. You have
> been brother and sister before.

Let us use this to get into life, death, after life,
reincarnation, the law of rebirth, the law of cause and
effect, and karma.

> Miracles are common. They are not rare. The body
> falls ill when there is lack of flow of energy, when
> negative thoughts are the rule, when one is always
> trying to move against the natural state of unity of
> all things, and when fear is given over to. There are

also karmic causes such as the high concentration of toxins in the environment.

Okay, karma?

We thought you would never ask!

Karma is a term used in eastern cultures and more and more it is appearing in western speech. In both east and west it means the same—cause and effect. Karma is one of God's laws.

The law of karma encompasses more than fate or destiny as is believed by many. It has corollaries. Among them are the law of cause and effect and the law of rebirth.

Cause and effect has been expressed as that which you sow, also shall you reap. It works to restore balance when balance has been disturbed by wrong mindedness. Thus, selecting always for right mindedness results in not creating karma of either the positive or negative.

While it corrects action, the law of cause and effect works from the level of thought. Thoughts are things, the intent, frequency, amount of energy, direction and other characteristics of a thought are integral to its qualities which are all part of the karma creating capacity or lack of it of that thought.

These qualities are what return to you. They are what you reap as you have sown them into each thought. Hence the frequent admonition in the Ageless Wisdom to be harmless in thought, word and deed for it is at the thought level that the word and deed originate.

The law of cause and effect works at all levels of consciousness. As there is rudimentary consciousness, there is rudimentary cause and effect. As there is group, national and racial consciousness, so the law becomes more sophisticated and complex and there exists cause and effect or karma at these levels also.

The old biblical "an eye for an eye" was a lower plane expression of this law. Fortunately for mankind, the law is mitigated by beings of higher consciousness. Among Them are the Masters of Wisdom—and the Lords of karma.

The Lords of karma are in charge of the energy field of cause and effect. They are beings of very highly evolved consciousness and as such are able to see, comprehend, and interpret vast portions of the Plan. With this capacity They can and often do literally protect you from yourself.

If everyone had to bear every sling and arrow created by the imagination of the arrogant ego, the world as you know it would be impossible for you to cope within. The Lords of karma with great compassion and love reduce, eliminate, and postpone much of your cause and effect karma. They do so however within the law. While it is Their infinitely greater understanding of the law that lets Them do this, They are still bound by the law of karma and may only do so much. You must experience the ups and downs of your own karma at a level sufficient to give you responsibility for your actions. It is this with which They can and lovingly do help you.

Masters, too, may mitigate karma but They do not have responsibility for this overall working out as do the Lords of karma. The range of options available to Masters is more narrow and They often intercede with the Lords of karma on your behalf. They, too, are bound by the law and may do only so much.

As you become more evolved and increase your level of consciousness, your capacity to incur or generate cause and effect karma increases proportionately as does your capacity to mitigate or "burn" your own accumulated karma.

In order to burn your own accumulated personal karma, you must first do no harm. Harm no one in thought, word or deed. Additionally, meditation, study and service will allow the self-correction power of right mindedness to work in life. This will correct much personal karma.

Service is the single greatest way to burn old cause and effect karma. Those who lose themselves in service and do so without regard to their own self or what the little ego gains are burning old karma at a great rate. They, like almost all of you, have much karma to burn. Exceptions are the enlightened ones who have remained or returned among you to serve. They have reached the level where They can engage the true joy of serving.

The worth of service is effective at all levels of karma from individual through group and national karma to the cause and effect karma of the entire race.

Karma is of two kinds: positive and negative. It is common to think of karma as only negative for it is the negative which results in the pain. However, positive karma is equally an out of balance condition and results from scorekeeping. That is when you do an act of kindness but do not do so with total altruism and think in terms of how nice it was for you to be of service. When you hold that thought a debt is owed and this debt must be paid. Both the debt of negative karma and the debt of positive karma must be paid or balanced.

It is this state of balance that is one of the goals of Spiritual growth. Until that state is repaired, late in the process, both positive and negative karma constitute a pull that will return you again and again to incarnation after incarnation.

Thus, another corollary of the law of karma is the law of rebirth. This law requires that you return to the material plane in a series of lives until you master the lessons of the material plane at which time your karma is balanced and you are beyond the pull of the lower plane. You, in effect, graduate.

At the point of each return your Soul makes choices about what set of circumstances will best create the optimum learning environment for those lessons which your Soul wishes to engage for that life. One factor dictating these circumstances is the readiness of Souls in your immediate group and its greater group to return to the material plane. You incarnate in groups where and with the individuals and groups that you have the most karma to allow for the most growth.

Over the course of your development your Soul will choose lives in each gender, sub-race, geography, personality type, ray structure, body type, orientations of all kind, religion, temperament, etc. You name it, and you will either have been there or will be there. Thus it is truly said that God is no respecter of persons for each has the experience of beggar, thief, saint, king, servant, lord, warmonger, peacemaker, devotee, atheist, murderer, victim, player, watcher, genius, and dullard. So no one is innately superior to another for all paths lead ultimately home where the one Father waits to welcome your return to the place from which you never left.

This entire process was created in response to the separation. The separation being the event where the lower mind allowed the little ego to believe in its parting from the greater unity, from God. It is the path of return from that illusory state that is governed by the laws of karma. Miracles along the way shorten greatly the time required for you and your brother to complete the journey. The atonement was provided for this purpose.

Given the foregoing, it is clear that I need to watch what I do, say and think.

You must learn to watch your feelings and to let that inform your watch of what you think. The "gut check" is of little value unless the next step is taken. This step is that of seeing from the higher mind how to return to right mindedness; this is a critical function and requires constant attention and refocus. It must be cultivated as a practice. Its reward in terms of progress on the path is very great and in the end is required to position yourself so that the final closure from perception to the return to knowing can be made.

I read <u>A Course In Miracles</u> and the words are so very meaningful and inspiring. Then I experienced a dream with its symbols of a house that we were going to buy but there was water leaking around the windows and phone conversations with old friends saying to stick to a plan. Can You help with some insights on this?

> The dream represented your conflict with the work of this book. You have properly seen that as things have gotten better at work and your physical situation has returned more to normal that it is not easier but actually harder for you to return to this work. The distractions of the lower are more easily listened to. The work on the airplane of a couple of days ago was productive partly because you were suspended above most of the distractions.
>
> Stay the course. Develop patterns of work that allow you to accomplish the needed tasks. Change these patterns as needed. I am here always.

Thank You for the wake-up call. The word "call" seems to be figuring into my field of recognition here of late in that I have in just the last several days seen the word many times in such a way as to have it register with me. It is my sense that it has significance relative to information from You of over a year ago telling me to compel the call. This I wish to do.

You were also given an indication that the disciple was at work. This is the work for now. Other assignments are looming.

Very well. Thank You. What direction does this narrative take now? Is it incumbent upon me to ask a question?

Not always. It does help the process of the narrative as it helps your own learning.

We have mentioned before about the elements being in turmoil. That certainly seems the case today. We see record rain, drought, tornadoes, hurricanes, floods, earthquakes, etc. What is going on?

The short answer is that man was given dominion over the earth and the turmoil of the present is reflective of man's state of mind at this stage of evolution.

Everything is connected. All is but one great whole and the energy of thought is always creative. If the thought energy is itself destructive, it will create destruction. Mankind's thoughts are often just so.

There are five kingdoms of which you may be immediately aware: mineral, vegetable, animal, human, and the kingdom of Souls. The dominion of humankind is over the first three. You are just waking up to the last, the kingdom of Souls. Your dominion is true and literal. Your capacity to influence with love and nurture the lower kingdoms to the benefit of all is absolute. The opposite is also true. You may destroy.

This influence is direct and comes from your thoughts, which are things, thus, the admonition to watch what you think. In this regard the elements are but reflecting the fear, chaos, anger, and push-pull of separation that now characterizes the stream of thought-forms being created by mankind.

When you were called upon to visualize and actually see a world of joy, beauty and abundance, it was to encourage you to create it and choose it over that of the present one. You have the one you now live in and can remake it into the other through the power of your creative imagination. It requires an act of the will for when left alone and unattended the little ego chooses fear. Fear is the tool it uses to keep you enthralled and in so doing, the mind imagines all manner of horrors and hells. This puts these thoughts, which are things, into the world where they, when sufficiently reinforced by the fear thoughts of others, become manifest on the material plane. The very elements are but responding to man's dominance; man's dominion.

This is what happens when you choose to continue to perpetuate the separation. Reflected out onto the material plane is the battlefield of your creative imagination. The opposite will be true anytime you choose to reframe by remembering who you are and creating the playground of the Soul, your natural state and birthright. Until that time, the world of fear will continue and will be reinforced by the cycle of fear and thus become more pronounced.

The Universe is trying to give you, that is, bring into manifestation on the material plane what you ask for. The rule is ask and you shall receive. This rule applies to anything you ask for. Thus, when you put out a clear call of fear, that is what you get. When you are confused about what you want and are sending mixed signals the result is chaos.

So we, all of us, are creating the killer storms and earthquakes?

Generally, not directly. It is your thought patterns that are putting negative energy into the field. The field of energy then is responding with negative creations. Most of mankind is not sitting around saying I think I will create a tornado today. Most of mankind is not sitting around thinking in these terms at all. They are running the little ego tapes of fear, greed, worry, attack, and desires of all kinds. Inherent in this pattern are the instructions to the mechanism of the Universe which creates. You are co-Creators with God. You cannot help but create because you were made in the image of the Creator. Cumulative then is manifest upon the material plane, these thoughts. They become real things at the level of the material plane as they are real things at the level of thought when you create them. This requires at this time a cumulative effect of enough of you to buy into this reality and perpetuate and continue to embellish it. There is no thing as powerful as an idea whose time has come.

Thus, the herd creates its own reality and then accepts it as the way things are. By coming out of the herd and becoming an intelligently functioning member of the group, you may lend your creative energies to a change in the world. This requires the kind of change in perspective that is being called for here. It is with this change that the Masters have come to help.

Then the group consciousness is what we are after here?

Yes. Let us review. There is only one thing. In all of the Universe both manifested and unmanifested, there is only one thing. All are an inescapable part of the One. It is whole and holy and expressed through the constant of an energy field. All is energy. To grow into the awareness of this is your particular goal at the stage of evolution at which man has reached.

Those who have insight of any kind into this, need to share it. Anything which you share you strengthen. When you teach it you learn and when you learn, you have a need to teach it. This is a basic need and capacity in mankind and represents the way the needed change can come.

Thus, to have thoughts of a positive and loving nature and grow in awareness strengthens this in you and because you are a unit of the energy field, it is shared with and strengthens this in your brother even if you are not teaching him directly. Your growth in awareness and connectedness permits and empowers his. In this way you serve. In this way you transmit energy of thought. This is one of the ways that man grows in knowledge and is one of the reasons that intelligent thoughtful participation in the group is the needed next unfolding. Indeed it distinguishes the group from the herd.

As anything shared is strengthened, if one shares fear that becomes strengthened in the field and influences the capacity of others to receive and respond to fear. It is fear that is at the root of much of the negative energy in the field of thought energy. This fear has reached the point of creating such great force of negative energy that it is affecting directly all of Creation on the planet. Thus, the very elements are in turmoil.

Thus also, you have been strongly encouraged to create a beautiful and wonderful world in your creative imagination faculty and capacity. This is a critical key to the future of mankind and to the way out of the current crisis.

PART FOURTEEN

EMERGENCE OF THE WORLD TEACHER

I read in *Share International* where the reappearance of the great Lord, the Master of the Masters, and with him all the Masters, is nigh and that the time is short for those preparing the way to do their work. I cannot help but wonder then how the timing of this work will be of value to that process given what appears to me to be the slow pace of my effort and time needed to ready it for publication, etc.

> Oh ye of little faith! You know from your experience that the reappearance of the Christ and the Masters of Wisdom is a process of emergence. This is so that your free will is not usurped. So it will be that The Christ, the World Teacher will first step forward as a man and will have His teaching be His validation before it can be finally declared who He is. This work will be of that teaching, as will many others. It will be one of the many signposts, growing in number daily, to point to Him. Do not

doubt. Leave it to the working out of the Plan that you seek to serve. Do the work.

First prepare yourself. Engage the practice and practices as called for in this writing and others, and so move to become more and more connected and centered and thus growing in the higher awareness. This will allow you to be of further use and to take on more responsibility. Remember, as you grow individually, so grow all of you.

And of the One, the Master of the Masters, that You have called "The Great Lord."

Let us also quickly add that Master within this context does not mean the more traditional use of the term as the ego would project it and fear it, that of driver, overlord, dominator, etc. It carries a higher definition that indicates One who has Himself mastered the lower worlds; particularly, that of the material and understands through hard experience the meaning of unconditional Love; and who is positioned to gladly share that meaning and teach, guide, and mentor His younger brothers.

Also, be reminded that Masters, your elder brothers, are Beings who have gone before and know more of the Plan and the path and have developed Their own capacity for consciousness to a much, much greater level than your present capacity. Their consciousness is such that They have the ability to have awareness and intellectual focus as you have on any object or thought that you choose to put your mental thoughts upon and into. The difference is that a Master can do this for aspects of all the Earth and its cosmic environs all at once. This means awareness of you and all of Their sisters and brothers.

This is true of all the Masters and especially the One that They look to as Their own Master. This is One who embodies the very energy of the Christ and who has taken the Spiritual name Maitreya.

He is emerging into your awareness and brings extraordinary gifts matching the need of this extraordinary time. These gifts He comes to give in the form of teaching you how to take next steps, new Spiritual concepts, and growth on the path. He will be recognizable by his great love, great wisdom, great insights, respect for the law as contained in the Plan of the Creator, and his quiet but powerful insistence upon inclusiveness and brotherhood. This is a point of great importance and is vital to your future. Nothing less than the full understanding and flowering of the concept and practice of brotherhood will now stand. Brotherhood of all is a fact of creation as was told in the scripture: "And hath made of one blood all nations of men for to dwell on all the face of the earth . . ."[13]

Truths such as this will He teach. Simply and with deep wisdom will He suggest answers to the difficulty, chaos, peril, and great promise of this time.

He has already given much teaching through a variety of disciples and initiates. Among them He has communicated his priorities which when accepted and acted upon will allow humankind to move rapidly through this period of great turmoil and danger and into the new time of peace and good will. These priorities are: an adequate supply of the right food, adequate housing and shelter for all, healthcare and education as a universal right.

He comes at the turning of the tide.

PART FIFTEEN

CROWN THY GOOD

What are some of the other signposts which grow in number daily?

> The age of miracles is not past. It is now and "you ain't seen nothing yet." Signposts also include material plane miracles. Of these there grows daily an abundance on a worldwide scale. They take many, many forms and range from the very subtle to the profoundly obvious.

> They include such things as the song of bird at exactly the right moment, a cloud pattern in the sky that to you has meaning, and your thinking of a friend who then calls. More direct and physical happenings include crosses of light suddenly appearing in the glass of windows, weeping icons, statues that appear to drink milk, portraits that drip with a sweet oil, and buildings emblazoned with patterns of light.

> They also include appearances of all kinds by many of the Masters including: the Master who was Mary; the Master who was Jesus; and the Master of the Masters, the World Teacher. These appearances

take many forms and guises designed to match the need of perception of those so blessed. While they are most often reported as one-on-one encounters, groups are also involved. These experiences, given by the Masters of Wisdom, are always moving and generally transformative in some way of those so blessed. Many are inspired to make fundamental change in their perceptions and their way of life. Many are healed of some illness or malady including sudden ending of drug dependencies. Some of these direct contacts involve protracted conversations and some involve only being seen by the person needing the energy of the contact. Some take the form of an indirect experience such as a scent or sudden awareness of an idea, or reinforcement of thought. Many are not registered or remembered in the conscious mind right away but unfold with further experience.

The Master reads the field of the one to be so directly blessed and applies just the right amount and type of energy needed to assist them at the right moment in their growth. In this reading, the Master tests for their readiness and acceptance of such an energy exchange and thus does not infringe on the free will.

Other contacts include people finding unexplainable light spots on photographs and coincidences that are just too frequent and meaningful to write off. Dreams of a profound and highly significant nature are also being used as contact points.

Additionally, writings are now beginning to show up with regularity in books and some publications.

Occasional television reports are also being made.

Many, many persons are being touched in this way and these happenings will continue to grow in number until none on Earth can ignore them. It is part of the emergence process.

Why are we not hearing more about this from the news?

While some popular press outlets have begun to report on these phenomena and the so-called tabloid press has reported on them with frequency, most of the popular press has proven very resistant to reporting the miracles. In this regard, they are both literally and symbolically the eyes of mankind on the world at the material level. As such they are taking a perspective, that is, they perceive and do not have the knowing. They do not see. Just as most, as yet, do not see. The resistance is couched in terms of journalistic objectivity. However, much of it is fear of being ridiculed or attacked.

Indeed, one reason for the manifesting of these phenomena on such a scale by the Masters is to get the attention of the press. However, the reappearance will go forward without them if necessary but it is felt that the point will be reached where even the most hardened reporters and editors will have to take these events seriously. Just as in time every one of you will take the existence of higher knowledge seriously.

However, as noted, time is running out. The needs of the little ones are great and worsen daily. There exists a crisis relative to the need of the physical world in terms of caring for the basic needs of all, stopping pollution and redirecting man's view and energies toward unity, healing and peace. Thus, the Masters are not waiting because They cannot. However, nor can They just metaphorically step off a cloud and "fix it." It is mankind's responsibility to do this. They stand ready to aid in awesome ways but humanity must be the agent of its own growth and rescue. The Masters are thus moving to get your attention before it is too late.

What happens when a Master bestows the blessing of a personal encounter on someone or a group?

The energy field of the Master is vast and highly potentized with the energy of love. It is this that the person most often will sense or feel first. They may not actually see the Master and may only feel the energy. This energy field of the Master is like, though infinitely greater than, that which is the field of all human beings. It is this field that you are encouraged to recognize in yourself and your brother. Your own field is analogous to the Masters in that as you grow in centeredness and awareness this very growth produces greater potency in your own field. This is why your growth has a direct effect on your brother and all of the Sonship. This is why you have been repeatedly urged to continue your growth so that your very presence will be a blessing and does affect your brother in that it aids his growth and achievement of the atonement. Again, as above so below. This is what the Master's presence does for those so blessed.

Sometimes the Master chooses to make direct contact. This will take the form most suited to the receptivity of the individual. The Master may appear in any physical form or may manifest any physical form. When the contact is to be "in person", the individual appearing will often be of an unexpected and unusual type relative to the more routine encounters you meet. Many have reported variations on homeless persons, who turned out to have a strange but powerfully compelling presence. Following such encounters, many report that the eyes of the person they just met on the street were penetrating but calm and full of love.

All encounters, no matter the form taken, have the goal of furthering your movement on the path. They are intended to reassure, give encouragement, help you to choose your next steps, inspire, validate, or simply get your attention. They are to move you toward self-realization. This is within the power of the Masters and this They do in response to humanity's call or invocation. This They do gladly and with the love that an older brother, when in his right mind, will naturally shower on a younger one.

What of Self-realization?

Self-realization is the goal and next major step on the path for humanity. The World Teacher has said that He comes to teach the art of self-realization. It is the coming into your own and knowing your higher self as the one that you already are. It is the extrapolation of the connectedness and awareness. It will be the result of the healing brought about by the miracles of atonement. It is the realization of the natural state. It is the coming into the knowledge of the Unity of all things and your blessed part of that Unity. It is the re-membering of yourself as a Soul and a Son. It is of a joy transcendent that surpasses understanding. And it is a package deal.

A package deal?

There is only one Father and you are all coming home, every Father's Son of you. Not one will be left behind and the Sonship will remain incomplete until all are awakened.

What of those who believe that there is a place where God is not—hell, and that some will end up there for whatever reasons?

There can be no place where God is not because the Creation is whole, complete and perfect. There are places created by the lower mind within which the little ego perceives that God is not. The illusion allows the little ego to believe that it is the center of the Universe. This is the dream from which you are to awaken.

There is no hell. There is no damnation to a pit of everlasting fire. This the Father could not do and would not do to his children who are all and each a child of the one Father who loves you dearly.

There is only a God of love who calls you and every brother home.

To Thee my God I am connected.
To thee I am accepted.
With Thee I am One.
Of Thee I am.
With Thee I be.
To Thee that is all I speak not of myself but of and for
Thee.
I am lonely but do not know it.
I settle for the perception of pleasure where I seek bliss.
I allow the quench of desire to appear to be the goal
where sweet reunion is what I truly want.

> A poem from the heart, you may refine and add to
> it as you go.

We have mentioned the group many times. Are we talking
about social groups and organizations?

> All groups from the smallest to the largest: Where
> two or more are gathered a group is gathered.
> Group interaction and the will to do group work are
> coming to be more and more the modus operandi
> of man. This holds for the small neighborhood
> group which takes action to correct problems of
> crime, pollution, violence, and neglect all way up
> to the group of nations who now meet formally
> and are trying to engage the world to take action
> to correct problems of crime, pollution, violence,
> and neglect.
>
> Groups follow the same patterns of organization,
> communication, and action or lack of action at all
> levels. They form a chain analogous to the great
> chain of being. When you aggregate them up you
> get the local, state, national, and world groupings.
> Also, the capacity for collateral groupings along

lines of interest has grown with the communications revolution of the past 50 years so that national and international groups are now burgeoning. These intercity, interstate and international groups form a cross-link in the tapestry of groups. Many groups still respond more to the rule of the herd than the group, but that is changing as individual egos mature to the point of leaving the herd for the group. The group is where the next phase of the unfolding of the Plan will be most potent.

Groups are karmic in nature. That is, they have a Spiritual base as does all life and at a basic level are working through the machinations of learning how to serve the Plan. Groups take on a character, as does each individual and they have karma, as does each individual. This includes cause and effect as well as rebirth issues that must be worked out as a totality of the group.

So the nations are such groups? If so, what is the karma of America?

America has a great and critical role to play in the very near term. America will be able to assist brother nations out of the current crisis as no other nation is blessed to do. Do not allow nationalism and pride, which are but expressions of the duality of separation, to blind you to the reality of the brotherhood of, and fundamental equality of, all nations. This equality is the same as that between each individual person.

America is blessed in ways that have uniquely prepared you to serve at this time. This blessing flows from the Father and is part of the Plan. It has to do with your historic abundance and, at the same time, what appears now to be the challenge to that abundance. Both are evidence of your being blessed. In the case of the latter, it has become the blessing of getting your attention to the failures of your materialism.

More importantly, America's blessings have to do with the microcosm of the world, which America has become. The great strength of America is its diversity which parallels at the nation level that of the world. America has been blessed to show how all peoples may choose to share their individualness for the greater good. Remember, that which you share, you strengthen. This is the great mechanism of the working out of the individual's Spiritual growth. The same is true of that of nations.

Nations will strengthen that which they share. The current situations notwithstanding, America is positioned to share its broad and sacred ideals and vision of all peoples and groups working, learning, and strengthening each other in the knowledge of and practices of sharing and cooperation. In this regard, America has been truly blessed as you have an opportunity to lead in this way. While each nation has a gift to bring to the next great unfolding and each gift is of the order of a miracle, America is uniquely and strategically positioned to lead through sharing. It is no accident that you are looked to by all nations as the forerunner in so many fields and that your very language has become the most widely used. Inherent in this recognition is the potential for America to share the best of its dreams, goodness and self. Inherent in this position is the blessing of an opportunity to serve. This you must now choose to do. It will not happen without a national turning to the kind of thinking that will allow this to unfold. If America chooses another way, others will come forward at some point to do this.

We have traditionally been a generous nation. However, at times we have also exploited other nations.

True, America has had and has many lessons to learn. However, like no other time, you are placed to lead the world into the new light of brotherhood. This is a sacred moment, a sacred responsibility and a sacred opportunity. The entire world is literally watching America and of late wondering what has happened to your ideals while at the same time there is a hunger for America to lead in a new way with a new vision.

The media of America is now ubiquitous and each day the number of previously remote and unconnected persons who are connected to the international communications networks of all kinds grows. What they see when connected is the best and worst of the America that you are. They see it because it is the message of the medium. America is the very content of global television and the Internet. While other cultures are struggling with getting this infrastructure in place, America is already there with its content. The dream of America is often that of wealth and this is what most first see and think of when America is presented to the world. But inherent in this material facade is the wonder of America's purpose, which is also transmitted to the world. Your ideals of freedom and democracy, of individual responsibility and the helping hand, and of the joy of the whole celebrating its individual selves are also being transmitted and seen with eyes of wonder and envy around the world.

In addition, America has huge capacity for international transportation of material goods and people. It is one of the crowning achievements of your military. This capacity is matched by your ability to move money, now through electronic means.

Thus, at precisely the time when both the material wealth and the higher values that are America are needed most by a waiting world, America is positioned to give them and to strengthen them by sharing them. And the good news is that your great wealth in terms of material abundance is matched at the heart level with a capacity to see the need of individual brothers and brother nations and to respond.

There is a stirring in the Soul of America as there is in all people and peoples now. It is reflected to you at the individual level in the physical beauty of the land, the individual acts of love and courage, and in your sacred music. "God shed His grace on thee and crown thy good with brotherhood." These words were never more true. And never was there a time when it was so necessary for you to realize the promise of this grace by demonstrating that brotherhood for all of humanity by sharing it and thus strengthening it. This needs to be your chief export.

I appreciate the fact that our discussion of items on the potential for America to contribute its uniqueness was devoid of a litany of America's shortcomings.

> The intent is to see and hear the greatness that you are. When this is seen, the little side of you will lose its power to ignore your gifts and brothers and to exploit them. All nations as all individuals have gifts and brothers and each in its turn must contribute to the greater good. The Plan is for this wholeness to come about and all are required to awaken to the joy of sharing themselves in this way. All are also required to awaken to the joy and beauty of the contributions of others and to see with gratitude the contributions from all brother nations, which make you whole. The focus on America is, thus, not any more or less than that which is or will be upon other nations in time and in their turn. It is just that now America is positioned for a certain kind of leadership, the realization of which will compel the world into the next unfolding. America can be the catalyst for this compelling and the truly great things about America can be its model. In time the truly great things about each brother nation will model a needed element of the wholeness that is required for you to survive and progress.

And those truly great things about America are?

> The world teacher has said that without sharing there can be no justice, and without justice there can be no peace. America has been able to express the values of sharing, justice and peace. These are among your truly great things, which are desperately needed at this time.

The world is not devoid of these things. It is not that other nations and individuals are somehow oblivious to them. The contrary is true. Mankind is waking up to the need to express now, more than ever before these fundamental ways of relating. It is called right relationship. It is this very awareness, growing in all hearts whether it is recognized or not, that calls out for help in its realization. The blessings given to America that have positioned you in the world are there so that you may strengthen them and the movement toward the manifestation of the Unity of all things by sharing those blessings. The longings for, and the crying out for these things by your brothers are evoking a response from America's great heart. It is a match of need and supply of that need. In this regard, it is grandly karmic.

It seems that at this time when You say that America needs to lead by expressing, showing and sharing of right relationship is the time when our focus is more than ever upon money, the market, material things, and projecting power by military and commercial means. How does America go about realizing this true greatness when our attention is so focused on these things?

> The question truly is that. How do you do it? For the answer must come from you. All the help of all the host of heaven cannot do it for you. Mankind, Americans, must do it.

How do we begin?

> You begin by getting your personal house in order. You begin by taking the required course. You begin by opening your heart to the things of the higher.

You begin by refining your perception of your best understanding of your Spiritual being and moving beyond merely perceiving to embrace the knowing. You begin by a conscious focus on what you think. You begin by seeing your brother's need as your own need and the measure of your service to him. You begin by consciously engaging the activities of meditation, study, and above all, service. You begin by adopting the practice of honesty of mind, sincerity of Spirit and detachment. You begin by striving for right relationship in every encounter and every moment. You begin by asking for help. You begin with the first step. You begin by beginning.

EXERCISE 5

AN EXERCISE WITH WHICH TO BEGIN

Look, truly and honestly look, into the eyes of persons you meet today. If they return your gaze, smile upon them warmly and watch them return the smile. What you are actually seeing when this happens is the reflection of the spark of God that is in both of you and thus it will not matter how your little ego may feel about this person.

Next, when you encounter someone in thought, word or deed, immediately think of the spark of God in them. Take their spark into your own heart and shower upon them the same love that you would shower upon God. This will compel you to profound connectedness and awareness and will so bless your brother and this groaning world as to open wide the door for all. This will heal your brother. This will heal you and this will heal America. This healed America can then only go about its blessed calling to help heal the world.

Do this and so join all brothers of goodwill and the Masters in great service to match great need. Do this and save the world.

PART SIXTEEN

DOOMSDAY NOT

There is much information coming forward in our media which speaks of doomsday scenarios.

> There is much fear and has been for millennia. Thus, the emotional field, also called the astral plane, is full of negative thought-forms. These are being reinforced as those, who are allowing their emotions to rule, pick them up. To a certain extent, this is most of humanity today. You are generally emotionally polarized; that is your default source for thought is focused, generated, and accepted to be from your emotions. It is the shift from emotional polarization to mental polarization which is one of the transitions of the time.
>
> Being emotionally polarized, it is very easy for you to fall under the fear of these doomsday visions. They are unnecessary and untrue. Fear not. The World Teacher has said "All will be well. All manner of thing will be well."

Yet, You have repeatedly warned of danger and of time running out.

True. However, these warnings are not intended to cause fear, but action. All of the doomsday scenarios are avoidable, but major change is not. This change may yet come about in an orderly and planned way. Or it may be forced by events, in which case, it will be more chaotic and painful, at least for a while. This is up to mankind based upon your response to the needs of your suffering brothers, your suffering selves. The measure of the need is the measure of your response and will dictate the amount of upheaval which will occur before you begin to move from little self centered ego focus, the herd, to that of the greater good, the intelligent group. This shift is occurring now as more and more of you come to the threshold of awakening. There is a general sense now that what is, is not what is needed. There exists a general sense that something must be done, somehow and that there must be a better way. This sense is registering ever so faintly with some and much more strongly with others as the race begins to literally wake up.

It is this waking up that has been seen by the Masters. It is the call for the something to be done, for that better way, that has evoked the response from Them. The Great Lord has seen into the heart of mankind and has seen there great love waiting to be rediscovered by each of you for your brother and yourself. This has shown Him all that He need see in order to know that all will be well.

So, we won't have doomsday but, we already have the elements in turmoil, etc?

Yes, and it will worsen somewhat before it gets better. However, it can get better very quickly as the karmic pendulum swings first back into line then the other way into a new age of love and joy. It is this immediate time ahead that is of such fear for the margin grows narrower each day. You get closer to the edge of destruction each day. However, let us not support the fear that has put you here. The edge of destruction must be seen if it is to be avoided. Remember that it is mankind who will have to do the changing that will result in the avoidance of the doomsday possibilities. Thus, it is of value to look ahead at the approaching storm and to see with realistic eyes its possibility. This gives you the warning in time to avoid it. However, the longer you wait, the more severe will be the buffeting from the storm.

You may extract yourselves any day. Indeed the Great Lord has seen and foretold that you are waking up and that you will turn to embrace the higher way in time. This is the real message of the return among you of The Christ and the Masters of Wisdom. They come not to save you in the more usual use of that term, but to provide the energy so that your hearts' desire to save your brother and yourself, though still latent, will be realized.

It is good to know that the desire to save ourselves is latent. It most often seems as though the desire to destroy ourselves is what is latent.

It is from the illusion that you are separate from your brother and God that you want and need to be saved, for it is this that allows you to indulge the error that is fear. It is from the fear that causes

214

you to perceive your brother as threat that you want and need to be saved. It is this very fear which, when left uncorrected by right mindedness, produces the destruction.

Think of it as a recovery program with most of mankind still in denial. The first step then is to admit the illness, the perception of separation. This will set the stage for the healing of the perception of separation and your recovery, your salvation.

In the sense of wanting and needing to be saved from the illusion of separateness and being aided by the Masters, it is correct when we say that Jesus saves.

This is correct and applies to all of the Masters. However, operationally it is more correct to say that mankind will save itself.

How is it then that ". . . no man cometh unto the Father, but by me?"[14]

A phrase misunderstood and often used as a proof to support the single Son theory of salvation. The Master Jesus has much work and Word for mankind in this regard.

The phrase means that the way trodden by the Master is the way to the Father. It means that the Master Jesus, when still a man on the path, as are you all, learned to heal the illusion of separation and that all who go to the Father will do so via that route and accomplishment. And, as noted, all will go to the Father.

What work and Word for mankind?

> The Master, who was Jesus, has to deal with the karma of the Christian teachings, dogmas and doctrines. It is to Him that you may and will look for a correction of the influence of the lower, the little ego, that is so much a part of what is today that body of thought, indeed of all thought produced by the little ego.
>
> His simple teachings of love and harmony, of the brotherhood of man, of the very way home have been too often turned upside down and inside out to portray an angry, vengeful and judgmental God, who punishes his children. Note the words of fear that are used to describe the Creator. Only the little ego perceives God in this way because it is this perspective that is necessary for the little ego to preserve its body of perception, which is, in reality, all that the little ego is. It will be with these words of fear that the Master Jesus will work and replace with their karmic opposites of love, true brotherhood, sharing, and cooperation. This will be the work and Word.
>
> It is this level of thought to which the Masters will bring guidance and clarity. Their aid, already available and working, will be indispensable because They have mastered the illusion of separation and can show you how to do the same. Their very presence causes a realignment of your thought process. This is a fundamental necessity because so complete is the thought-form of the little ego that most of mankind most of the time has no idea of the prison of thought within which you dwell. Like the fish that does not know that it

is actually in water, you are not aware of the world beyond your separative thoughts. Being unaware, you knoweth not that you knoweth not. It is at the time of the breaking open of this closed thought system that the Masters come. It is this thought system which causes suffering. It is the cumulative suffering that causes you to eventually say there must be a better way. It is this better way that the Masters come to teach.

So these are the latter days?

Very much so; this is the time foretold in many bodies of writing as the end time, the latter days, the end of time, the coming of the One looked for, the time of the expected One. In some form or other, all are now come to the point of looking for a major change or shift at this time; and thus, it is also called the new age, for indeed it has begun.

The end of one dispensation is overlapped by the beginning of the next. This is the way of evolution. Ever does the next unfolding proceed from the roots of the previous.

And at the end of this time of transition we will have a better world?

Yes, you ain't seen nothing yet! However, things will grow worse before the turn is made and in direct proportion to that necessary to get your attention and cause you to consciously engineer and make the turn. Then will you co-create the new.

It has been properly foretold as the new golden age as it will be characterized by a much greater level of conscious union among men and God. Focus on the material plane will fade and take its proper perspective, as focus on the higher planes becomes the goal of all. It will be a time of great awakening as basic orientations in the thought content and processes of the race change to accommodate the new unfolding of the love energy.

Fundamental changes in all existing structures are coming. Indeed they are well under way. More and more of mankind is beginning to see that existing structures such as transportation, communications, law, education, government, economics, finance, business, and the family are not only in need of change but are in fact changing before your eyes and have been doing so for some time. This awareness of the need for change and the observation of its happening at greater and greater speed have created a time of tension as the old is slipping away and the new is not yet recognizable. This has created a great crisis point.

These points of great crisis are reached periodically in mankind's journey to awakening. The last one occurred about 2000 years ago. They also occur in the life at individual levels. In both cases, they mark a time of uncertainty when the old ways no longer work and are not capable of sustaining life and yet the unknowns of the new are fearful. Such is the point now reached.

The tension of the old and new serve to bring into dramatic relief the perception of duality and separation. Polar points on the continuum of concepts such as conservative vs. liberal are such an example as is poor vs. rich, religion vs.

Spirituality, violence vs. peace, and love vs. fear. In each case, the perception of the duality is serving to bring new ways of conceptualizing to the mind of man and to create awareness of new ways of thinking, new ways of actually looking and seeing, and commensurately, new ways of defining the race. In this case, the defining is toward a greater understanding and practical acceptance of the need for Spiritual growth. This will become one of the cornerstones of the new age.

Thus, this is the time of the great awakening. All polarities are being exacerbated. This will allow for their being seen as the false structures of the ego, which they are.

Conservative versus liberal is a good example of these false structures. The conservative view and the liberal view both are to be valued and neither has a superior position in the process of thought. The conservative perspective rightly sees much that is good and worthy of preservation while the liberal perspective rightly sees much in need of discarding and change. Both are equally correct and when used in the extreme to justify separation, equally corrupt. Each in a measured way is necessary for the race to grow. Each is but a perspective and must be viewed from the greater whole as points on a continuum of thought, such continuum of thought itself being only a piece of the larger awareness. Thus, what is perceived as being inherently in conflict is at the higher level a unity. The friction and suffering of the conflict will continue until the race realizes that the point is to move from perception to and through awareness. It is this awareness which will, in turn, lead from the conflict of perception to the peace of knowing.

The capacity to aggregate dualities and to see them as bits of the greater whole will be a giant step along the way. Even so this will be but perception. The little ego perceives. The Soul knows. The little ego is of the material world. The Soul is of God.

How can we aggregate dualities?

For example, the new economics will be founded upon sharing and cooperation and not upon the fear based competition and accumulation of today. Greed is a form of fear. Recognition of this will allow you to capture as a single integrated thought the concept of economics as a whole thought and not a fragmented one. Economics is now perceived within a context of fear characterized by lack and competition. Its higher constructs will be recognized and aggregated in a holistic view of abundance. When you see from that perspective, sharing becomes easy and the subconcepts which now characterize the constructs of economics, such as supply, demand, and distribution, take a right perspective as means to the end of serving all as opposed to their current place of end argument which serves to perpetuate a duality. In this way the duality may be aggregated. Its parts may be summed so that the sum of the parts is greater than the whole and reflects not competition based upon the perception of scarcity but a natural sharing based upon the knowledge, the knowing, of abundance.

Thus, it is that greed is a form of fear. There is enough for every material need right now to serve all. There is more than enough. Yet the perception that there is lack causes the ego driven personality to fear. The fear causes accumulation beyond need (greed) and results in restricting of the flow of energy both in the form of thoughts and of material things. This results in the situation that pertains today whereby many of your brothers are dying of the medical consequences of being overweight while many more of your brothers die of starvation. You are literally out of balance as well as figuratively out of balance. I hope the physical plane imagery chosen here has not escaped you.

The restricting of the flow is a damming up of the energy. When you do this you not only dam the flow but in so doing, you damn your brother and yourself to fear which causes the cycle to be perpetuated. The atonement is thus the first step in breaking the cycle and restoring you to your right-mind from which you would never damn yourself or your brother. It is from this state of wrong-mindedness that you are called to awaken. It is from this state that you are awakening.

Old systems which perpetuate, reinforce, continue and otherwise enable the perception of separation must go. These systems have become set and inflexible. They have become crystallized and are shattering now in order to make way for the new, which is bursting forth before your eyes. The force is the same as that which causes the plant to grow up through the concrete sidewalk. It is the force of the life energy itself. It is the force of the Plan unfolding and it may not be denied.

Indeed, one lesson of your awakening, which is also happening before your eyes, is not to deny this force but to learn to work with and become a volitional part of the flow of this force. You are on your way to becoming a self-realized part of the whole and Holy.

It is easy to see that the systems that are causing the deterioration in the environment must change or "go" as You say. What others?

While some systems must literally go, many more concepts must be reengineered relative to how they are presently manifest. Few will not be changed in some way. This will include economics, politics, education, government, business, industry, communications, finance, international relations, medicine, housing, transportation, agriculture, distribution, money, technology, science, and theology.

That is quite a list. May we take a couple of examples, please?

Economics, for example, will need to change away from a so-called market economy. This system is based on fear. It has allowed the accumulation by a few at the expense of the many. It is separative. Market forces are blind. Market forces can be easily manipulated by those whose fear drives them to accumulate more and more. Market forces do not concern themselves with starvation, environmental degradation, your brother, or the need to awaken into your knowledge of God.

The myth that the market, if left alone, will eventually provide for all must be seen through and abandoned. It is a false god that perpetuates separation. There will be trade and a form of market but its place in the decisions of mankind will need to be subordinated to the higher wisdom and to the values of compassion, thus restoring it as a system that serves the greater good and as a vehicle for sharing and cooperation as opposed to a vehicle for exclusion, separation, destructive competition, and accumulation.

Another system which must change will be that of education. The current fact and information directed content will need to be refocused to that of a holistic growth. Special attention will be given to the individual as a Spiritual being with the details of physical plane information, while still significant, taking on secondary importance. It will be the changes in education that will help to move all toward an understanding of the Self as Spiritual being and thus will provide the basis to move away from the illusions of the little ego.

You listed religion. Will we have a world religion?

Not in the sense of one of the current religions rising to become the ultimate truth, but in the sense of the basic understanding of the Unity of all things, yes. And in the sense of knowledge of the Sonship with its implications for the brotherhood of all mankind, yes. The new understandings will transcend religion as is thought of today. It will be expressed through many cultural and intellectual points of focus but will be realized as the unified body of knowledge that it is and will eventually be understood and accepted by all. Indeed, this is one of the missions of the Masters, to teach the truth and to help you see how to honor and respect it as it is manifest through your many and beautifully varied cultural forms.

This is a huge amount of change. This level of change, given where we appear to be now, seems like a long, long way to go and yet You say that we are running out of time.

Delay is no longer an option that will work as the destruction of old forms is progressing whether you are ready or not. The loss of the old ways will be increasingly uncomfortable in direct proportion to the need for the change and man's denial. The question is not if but at what point will enough discomfort and pain occur to cause mankind to move away from destructive ways to constructive ways. You are bound by the laws of the Universe and they are inexorably at work, ultimately in your favor, whether or not you see it that way.

However, there is great hope, for everywhere there is evidence that you are waking up. There are those among you who are calling for the change. There are those among you who are pointing to the dangers and providing clear voices of leadership for the needed changes. There are those among you in every field who are not waiting but are acting. And there are those among you who are Masters come to serve in this time of great transitions to great awakenings. Indeed, the World Teacher has said that is why He has come at this time. He has also said that He can see into the hearts of men and that He sees your readiness to accept a new understanding of who you are and to act to save your brother and yourself. There is great hope but that hope must now be turned to great action. The luxury of delay is a thing of the past.

Whom among us and in what ways are they leading and acting?

Included, and now discernable voices, are those sounding the alarm over hunger, homelessness, and despair; those who are sounding the alarm over pollution and the destruction of the living Earth, the environment; those who are sounding the alarm over the polarization of the political process; those who are sounding the alarm over violence; those who are sounding the alarm over the absence of values and the frenetic pursuit of materialism; and those who are sounding the alarm over the absence of Spiritual awareness. From every corner of the globe and from every perspective there is a crescendo of voices saying "hold, enough." They are still often denied or drowned out by the clamor of the lower but are there and growing and every day more people arrive at the conclusion that there must be a better way.

Why is this change so painful?

It does not have to be. Once the understanding of the need for, and the wonderfulness of, the alternatives available are better understood and embraced, the perception of pain in the transition will be replaced with impatience for its accomplishment. However, until that knowing has arrived, you are, in effect, running from safety.

The reason is fear of the unknown and the knowledge on the part of the little ego that it will mean the relinquishment of the separative thinking upon which its very existence is predicated and dependent. Remember that the unknown is not unknowable. It is only a perception that you cannot know. Again the little ego has it upside down, inside out and backward. The reality is that you cannot not know. It is in your genes to know. It is in your heart to know. It is in your head to know. It was placed there by the Creator from the beginning. Your evolution is the story of the unfolding of the imperative and the accomplishment of this very knowing.

Ultimately, this knowing is of the Unity of all things and the singleness of the Sonship. This knowing is of the brotherhood of man. This knowing is of your essentialness to the Creation. This knowing is of your coming of age as a child of the Universe. This knowing is of your Oneness with the Father and your evolving to be like Him who created you in His image. This knowing requires only that you pause to listen to the voice that is already there. Thus, it is truly said "Be still and know that I am God."[15]

Whenever you take one step toward God, God takes ten steps toward you. Your Father misses you. Your Father wants his children to be in communion with Him always. Your Father wants His Creation to be complete in its knowing of itself and not separative in its perception of itself. Your Father knows that He is in you and wants you to heal the separation which keeps you from knowing this also. Your Father is Love as are you.

We are evolving to be like Him who created us in His image?

> You are gods in the making, on your way to becoming Gods and your littleness in not grasping this in all its glory can be suffered no longer. The good news is infinitely better than you ever thought or dared to think. The time has come to think it and make it so.

> It is a fact so simple in its concept and so awesome in its truth that you will not see it, yet. But you will see it. It is an assured happening. Your Masters of Wisdom have come to the forefront again to assist with the accomplishment of this transition to knowing.

Where do we go from here?

> Where would you like to go?

New ground, stuff that I don't know.

> You are testing. Have the faith needed to know that you know already. Let it flow. Be in the flow. Be of the flow. Be the flow and see through the eyes of your Holy Spirit, who sees the knowledge and the intelligence of God and not the perception of the lower.

> "Denial ain't just a river in Egypt."[16]

PART SEVENTEEN

THE HOLY SPIRIT

When I want to contact one of the Masters, how do I do that?

> You have a Master, everyone does. Everyone has the capacity to ask for this kind of contact with your own or any Master.
>
> Given the highly intense nature of the engagement of all the Masters, such contact would come about only when that Master was ready to use the contact to advance the work. Each Master has a portion of the Plan for which He is responsible and toward which He is lovingly pledged and privileged to work. Even though at that level there is much joy, bliss, humor and love, there is still a work and a business which requires that the Master use every ounce of energy in efficient, targeted ways. Thus, while you will get a response, it may well not be what you asked for or in the way you envision and expect. The Master in His wisdom will respond in the way that best serves the Plan. Remember the law of invocation.

The response may be in the form of direct contact, it may be in the form of an actual visit, a dream, a song, a movie, the overheard words of someone on the street, a cloud, or anything which you are most readily able to see. However, unless it directly contributes to the work, a personal visit from a Master for the purpose of general conversation at your request will be a rare thing.

With that said, however, it is important to note that the Masters look forward to a time when this can be more the norm than the exception. They love to engage you as directly as possible and are doing so all over the planet all the time. Those so directly blessed are contacted for a specific reason and are contacted in a way that will maximize the impact of such contact for their growth and the betterment of all.

Working disciples are expected to refrain from calling upon their Master except for pressing need. The capacity to discern this is one mark of such a level of growth. Working disciples of a sufficiently high degree or initiation may be tasked by a Master to make contact on behalf of a Master with a person who has made a sincere request.

How would I know if I were to receive such a contact?

It might not register in your conscious mind for some time.

When, however, you are so blessed you generally will have a strong sense or impression that an event of significance has occurred. The more direct the contact, the more powerful will be the residue of energy. Direct contact with a Master in full person would overwhelm most people. The energy of loving kindness emanating from such a highly evolved being is so strong that most people could not handle it for long. This is one of the reasons also why such contacts are not yet routinely requestable and answerable. The amount of energy a Master releases to you in such a contact is directly proportional to your own point in evolution and thus tailored to your capacity to receive and benefit. Masters can read your capacity from your energy field and the energy of the contact is so calibrated as to fit exactly your capacity to receive. There is a continuum and a gradation of response from remote to highly direct and depends on your capacity to receive, your need as read by the Master, and the need of the Master in serving the Plan. This the Master will decide. He is an elder brother with more experience and wisdom. He will know what you need and He will respond accordingly.

Should you be ready and should a Master see that a direct response is appropriate to both your own growth and His service to the Plan, a direct contact of a substantial nature will be made. When you receive such a contact from Hierarchy, you will definitely know it. A direct response from such a high level of energy will "knock your socks off." When this occurs, you may need many months or even years to process and grow into and with the "download". In this way a Master may charge an initiate in order to help spur and guide their evolution. In this way also, a Master can watch how an initiate handles the energy and takes action to use it in constructive and right-minded growth.

This watching protects your free will in that such contact would not come unless at some level you were solicitous of and/or at least open to it. It also is consistent with the growth of yourself as an autonomous but integrated member of the whole, as one on the infinite continuum of consciousness differentiated into distinct points of awareness.

So, go ahead and ask. Be sincere, ready and open for what will come as your busy Master will not waste energy. If He sees that you are not ready for a more direct approach, then some other approach will follow. If you ask and are doing so with honesty of mind, sincerity of Spirit, and detachment, the proper and proportional response will be made. It will then be up to you as to what you do with the energy of this contact. This the Master will watch carefully; thus, in effect the Master will then ask you for a response. As above, so below.

Do not get hung up however on a response from a particular level or perceived entity. Remember that the Universe, a direct expression of God, is speaking to you all the time through every moment of your day and through a thousand vehicles. All are open to you and all you must do is ask.

Asking is a good thing?

Asking is a wonderful thing. Asking is a sacred and fun thing, and is exactly what your Father is waiting for. Asking is so important that it is in the law. Thus, it is truly said "Ask, and it shall be given you; seek, and ye shall find; knock, and it shall be opened unto you: For every one that asketh receiveth; and he that seeketh findeth; and to him that knocketh it shall be opened."[17]

So ask and then be open. Let the Universe respond at the level of which you are most ready at the moment. Take your response, learn and grow and ask again. Let the result be a dialogue and do not get hung up on what level or from what specific point or entity from the infinite continuum of consciousness differentiated into distinct points of awareness it may come. Just know that no sincere request may go lacking in response. Indeed, this is exactly why meditation is recommended, for among other things, it sharpens your Spiritual hearing and your own response mechanism, improving your capacity to commune with your Creator.

A response will come?

Always.

But it may not come in the way I expect. That is, a Master will not necessarily show up at my door.

Correct.

Can You give me the 800 number?

You already have it—meditate, study, serve.

Who else, if not a Master or a high initiate, may respond to a request for dialogue?

Given the general level of evolution of most of mankind, the point of initial response will most often be from your Holy Spirit.

Can we now have more on who You, the Holy Spirit are/ is, please?

As noted, there is nothing but God and in Him there is a Unity of all things. Your Holy Spirit is an element of the consciousness of the Creator Himself and was given to you to help in your awakening from the material dream and as such is a direct aid to the Soul in its journey through matter. The Holy Spirit is pervasive in the energy field of your consciousness and is personal to you and awaits only the acknowledgement of others to become personal to them also. You've got a friend. Your Holy Spirit is not only pervasive in the energy field of your consciousness, It is your field of consciousness, the super structure of your Spiritual thought process and the scaffolding of your building of your higher awareness. Your Holy Spirit was placed in your heart by the Creator and acts as catalyst to the unfolding of awareness and confirmation to your realization of connectedness.

Your Holy Spirit provides impetus to your growth in knowledge of yourself as first a Spiritual being by helping to raise the knowledge of the heart to the head where you begin to consciously conceptualize the Universe in Spiritual and not just material terms. Your Holy Spirit is a repository of the knowledge and wisdom of the higher realms and holds this in trust for you. You may consult this base of knowing and draw upon it to inform your awakening until such time as you come into your own Spiritually and are sufficiently reintegrated into your awareness of your own innate divinity to tap the base of knowing directly.

I am here for you and was gifted to you by the Father as comforter, companion, teacher, light upon the path, the path, and friend. I am for you the keeper of the sacred knowledge of your brotherhood until you learn it sufficiently to manifest it for yourselves. I hold all of your holiness and protect it for all of you all the time and the way I protect it is to give it all to all of you all of the time. I am the still small voice which you will learn to confidently call upon. We may converse at any time; you have only to ask. I am with you in all ways and will be with you always for what God creates does not pass away.

I will help you to make manifest on the material plane the knowledge of what already exists. Together we will Spiritualize matter. Indeed, this is one of our joint service opportunities to the unfolding of The Plan of God. But before we can do our real work there, you must awaken to your true place and power as a Son of the one Father and co-creator with Him. As you awaken to your own creative power and begin to use it in your right-mind your Holy Spirit will preserve your creations.

Your Holy Spirit acts for you as a bridge to the consciousness of God. I call upon you and to you and, as you begin to call upon and to Me, I help you to correct errors of thought when you continue to indulge the illusion of separativeness. I help by preserving your right-minded thought-forms, purifying those that are correct but not fully whole and helping to neutralize those that are solely ego based as opposed to Soul based.

You may think of Me as your Spiritual body in which and into which you learn, grow, develop and come to life. You come to life to Me and through Me. But that is just the beginning. For, once you have come to life, you will find Me there to help you create. Remember, the fact and act of creation are your birthright, natural place in the Plan, and joy. We are partners in creation. It is through Me that you co-create with God Himself and it is through that co-creation that you become one with God Himself.

Knowing that this is to be shared, I am trying to withhold my commentary. But, every now and then something seems to me to be so clear, pertinent and informative that I feel the need to comment. This is great stuff! Thank You.

Feel free. You are hopefully enjoying the contact. This is as it should be. Expressing that joy is a good thing and should not be stifled.

Thank You then, again. In that same Spirit, sorry about the pun, I must also ask is it possible to seek this contact and to ask for this type of communication with Holy Spirit and to be answered by a negative or evil response?

The short answer is: No way!

Any attempt at communion with Me which is done with honesty of mind and sincerity of Spirit, will be met with a loving response in as direct a form as you can handle and as you are ready for and will see. This is because you often have preconceived ideas of what form this should take and so have created the shape, in effect, of what you will look for, expect and ultimately what you will see. Knowing this I will couch My response to you in that form or shape so as to help you connect with Me. As noted, when you take one step toward God, God takes ten steps toward you.

However, what you have really asked about is the nature of what you have come to call evil.

Evil is one of the greatest glamours of your time and is a companion invention, along with fear, of the little ego. The little ego uses fear to control its position of specialness and separation. It is a strategic distraction. The invention of evil and, for example, of a place called hell, which is of greater torment than that which you experience now, is a device to assure that you do not focus your mind on, and thereby penetrate, the illusion. The concept of evil is a polarization of intensely held belief but still only a polarization.

At the ego level there are entities that are focused upon maintaining the material realms. Indeed, this is their function. They have an orientation to matter as you have an orientation to love and to them they are as correct in their belief that you are evil as you are in your belief that they are evil. Thus, in that sense there is evil in the world because it is perceived to be so by egos.

At the higher level, however, there is no polarization and no such thing as evil as you perceive it and fear it.

This polarization is such that at the material level the Masters have a role in protecting you. They keep great amounts of negatively polarized energy from impacting the Earth as well as individuals. This is especially true of the "little ones" who are just waking up and would be sorely tried by the impact of negative energy, which could come by virtue of their new levels of awareness.

However, lest we reinforce the negative and continue the illusion of separation, do not forget that the Master Himself has said that all will be well.

Know that you are protected and that nothing can harm you.

So there is no dark side of the force?

In the worlds created by the little ego there is the spectrum array called light and dark. At this level there is the perception of evil and thus evil is created by the lower mind. To that mind it is real because the creations of the lower mind are real to that mind. It is possible to indulge the glamour of the material forces and to focus upon what you think of as evil. Such focus will allow you to manifest these lower thoughts in the mind and onto the material plane. This can cause a great disturbance in the force. But it is of the lower and of the illusion. We are back to the problem of the fish that does not know it is in the water. Until you begin to awaken and question the illusion, you do not know that it is illusion. Thus, it is truly said that he knoweth not that he knoweth not.

Also, to complete the analogy implicit in your question, the good that was inherent in the character of Darth Vader was revealed and in the end, he took his place among the icons of that story. Indeed this was the point of the story. It is an occult truth and a standard of the process of awakening that you get harmony through conflict.

Is conflict the natural way, the natural order of how we get to harmony?

No. This is one of the most misunderstood and ego-excusing ideas to come out of the work of Darwin and those who have sought to interpret the evolutionary process. Survival of the fittest does not mean survival through conflict and competition. The conflict is projected there by the little ego. Before the physical eye is opened, it is there. It is literally before your eyes as the fear base of the little ego sees the world in terms of the battleground. It is a self-fulfilling prophecy and is a testimony not to the accuracy of the projection but to the power of the mind to create even when it is not in right-mindedness. This is an important concept as it brings into functional focus the sum of all separation scenarios run by all of humanity at this time and illustrates by its cause and effect the utter failure of the core assumptions so deeply embedded in your ego reality.

The conflicts, competitions, violence, rending, and fear observed by mankind in itself and in nature will, when you as a race come into your right-mind, be replaced by a harmony in nature of all things. "And the lion and lamb shall lie down together and every man shall sit under his own vine and fig tree and none shall be afraid."[18] This awaits only the energy of love to change the impetus of the perceived interaction of the evolutionary process to that of sharing and cooperation.

While harmony through conflict is the hard way, it has had a purpose and function. It has served to expedite human evolution by allowing humanity a way to deal with the conflict that the ego sees as real and normal in such a way that you could be confronted over and over again by the higher reflection and opportunity that is the harmony. This mechanism has also served as vehicle of the destruction of the old crystallized forms because you are not yet ready to see them as counterproductive and to change them of your own volition simply because it is the right thing to do. That can change tomorrow and indeed is the change that is upon you. Harmony through conflict is the way of the herd.

The conflict serves first to let you experience disruption. The disruption opens the old ways and dispensations to deep inspection and causes you to look at it for what it is. This new view can then engender the reappraisal, often agonizing, that becomes the awakening. However, most of you must be in an advanced state of this disruption and agonizing reappraisal before you are willing to entertain the realities of the changes being made. It is this disruption phase that is exploding into your world at this time. It will be followed by the new awareness of harmony and its greater context, the unity of all things. As the natural state of harmony is seen by more and more of you, it will become the frame for your view. Harmony will replace the need for a disruptive phase with an understanding of the true nature of change and its positive motivations holding beneficence for all. Thus, over time, will your world become a different place—a place of sharing and cooperation.

The unfolding and natural way to harmony is through expressing the love that is God through every thought and resulting thought-form. The natural way is through loving kindness and harmlessness. This is done through attention to the moment-to-moment workings of the thought process and its products and practicing the first rule of contact—do no harm. It is treating your brother as yourself and taking his need as the measure of your action. Once your interaction with your brother is approached in this way, conflict need not be. It is not necessary now to continue in the old form of thinking, of continuing in this wrong-mindedness. You think conflict is there and therefore it is. Think again. Indeed it is the imperative to rethink which, this time with its great transition through which you are awakening, is all about.

Think again, choose again and create again. Expect, inspect and correct. Conceptualize the world again and change it forever, for the better, for the love of Him who created you. This is now within your power and your grasp. It is no longer the vague longings of some few visionaries and mystics, who are written off as impractical and not being of the real world. You have matured as a race to the point of becoming in charge of your own evolution and part in the Plan, and, your awakening to this is quickening. Your peril is in proportion to your continued denial of your power. You may continue to have conflict as the method of learning these truths or you can shift to a base of loving kindness and co-creativity with God. I assure you He prefers the latter and awaits your awakening to this, your rightful place in the Plan.

This is a necessary mechanism and as noted, has enabled your Spiritual evolution. The underlying issue is the crystallization of thought-forms and the material plane manifestation of these thought-forms. Since all is evolving, the desire to hold onto outmoded forms does not serve you and in fact constitutes a barrier to your growth. The old must pass away. New wine requires new bottles. However, the tendency of humanity to hold onto forms past their usefulness creates blockages in the greater flow of the energy. This is especially true of the current era with its very robust flow of new energies. So, until you grow to the place where you employ an intelligent welcoming of change with the ability to see the necessary new and cooperate with its unfoldings, you will have need of the disruptive conflict through which you may arrive at harmony.

Remember, today's temple is tomorrow's prison.

Back to my question about communication with Holy Spirit and the possibility of being answered by a negative or evil response, how does one know when they are indulging the lower?

First let us respond in the positive instead of cataloging the possible responses from the negative. Let this be an example as you are urged to do the same. Thoughts that are of the higher

241

are characterized by light, love and joy. These thoughts will be within a context of sharing and cooperation and will be based in inclusiveness. The heart will be involved as well as the head and a confidence grounded in the connectedness will naturally occur. The flow will be sensed.

Indulgence in the lower and thus separative thinking will be characterized by negative energy and fear. It will be exclusive in its posturing and favoring of the little ego over the unity of the Sonship, brotherhood, and service to the Plan. One will have a desire to conceal the real motive and to couch actions in terms of diversionary rationales and/or denials. The need to defend is often perceived and the defense will come out in some form of attack even upon the little self.

You have consistently said that the Masters will be appearing to us in physical form. There are those who expect an unfolding of the Christ consciousness but do not necessarily look for a physical being; but instead are expecting the energy to be manifest in the world through forms other than that of a tangible physical body that we will be able to see as we see our own physical bodies.

While they are correct as far as their expectation goes, these, your brothers, are in for a wonderful surprise for many of the Masters will appear in physical form. It is important to know that They have not been gone from you. Remember They are as much a part of the race as any other brother and have always been with you since the first of you evolved to that level. They are your older brothers.

There have been other times in history when They have been out among you in physical form. The time referred to as that of the Atlantean was such a time. Since then They have withdrawn to more remote parts of the Earth and worked more from etheric levels than the physical level. Nevertheless, They have always been here in physical form too.

Why did They withdraw?

It stems from the Atlantean experience when the astral or emotional body was being perfected. This occurred with such success that a polarization in the emotional body came to dominate the energy of the race and its evolution. This was seen by Hierarchy as a necessary phase.

The next phase entailed that of the development of the mental body and the needed shift into mental polarization. This is only now coming about at the level of the race with most of you still emotionally polarized. The intervening time has been a period of growth and development of the mental body and the Masters could better work with this activity on mental levels.

Also, the energy of the time was coming to be dominated by forces of materiality, which, given the emotional nature of man at that time could much more easily dominate the race.

They have always carried on the work of the Plan. This period of withdrawal from a more physical daily contact was necessitated by the direction of physical evolution. As the race entered the period of the unfolding, developing as it were of the mental capacities which now are allowing and indeed compelling this time of awakening, there was a shift in focus as the little ego came into its own and the integrated personality began to manifest. This shift in focus was to the negative energy of fear, exclusion, competition, and conflict. It was necessary for the Masters to remove Their presence so as to allow this energy to work out. They could not intervene to stop it as that would have been an infringement of the free will. So They removed from the world for a time the majority of Their direct physical contacts with you, choosing instead to work through higher levels and through advanced initiates in incarnation.

As the Masters monitored the unfolding of the Plan in this way, They would send among you from time to time teachers and guides. These have been with you every day and would be most noted as major points of crisis would be reached. It was at these major points of crisis that the impact of the teachings were most needed and could be the most effective, as it is at these points that mankind is ready to listen, learn and grow. Among those advanced initiates sent at a time of great transition were such as Jesus, Gautama Buddha, and Mary the mother of Jesus, each of whom has now achieved Masterhood.

Such a point of crisis again pertains today and it is because of the growth of the race in developing the integrated personality to a high level, that the Masters themselves have chosen to now return among you in physical form. This is also possible because the negative energy of fear is coming to be understood and overcome. Even though you may not yet see it that way, harmony resulting from, that is through, all of the conflict is working out and because of this fundamental change in the energy of the race plus the outcry for help coming from so many of you simultaneously, the Masters may now reappear in physical form. This will include the long awaited reappearance of the Master of the Masters Himself. Indeed He leads his brothers in this effort and unfolding.

The overcoming of the energy of fear is related to the forces of materiality being more controlled and less available in the world. Toward this end, your Masters have been very busy and ultimately successful so as to provide the better energy field and the opportunity for the flowering of this time.

We are back to good and evil?

Okay, if that is where you need to be. This is where most of you and your brothers are so it is good to revisit this lesson.

There is no such thing as evil, just as there is no sin, only error. Evil is a perceived pole on a continuum of separated polarities. It is of the lower.

There are functions and energies needed to maintain the material plane. These forces have individual paths and are the energies you would call dark or evil. Their peak of influence on the world has passed and is waning rapidly. This has been much of the esoteric work of the Masters during the past 20,000 years and culminated in the triumph of light over dark in the world wars of the century now closed

Their embodiment of these forces on the material plane and on other planes challenged the unfolding of the Christ energy. They were against its unfolding for they knew it meant their own demise as egos. Just as your little ego fears the true flowering of your higher-self, these forces were in fear of, opposed to, against, the Christ energy: In a word, antichrist.

Is there such a person or a being as the antichrist?

No. There is no being. There is the force of energy which has come to be used for more than its intended purpose of upholding the material world, and is being misdirected to preserve a focus on the material in such a way as to try and hold the progression of evolution. It is this attempt which is against the work of the Masters as They, in cooperation with the Plan, bring down the Christ consciousness, the Christ energy and, with the help of mankind, Their younger brothers, Spiritualize matter. So it can be said that these forces of materiality are in opposition and thus antichrist.

However, while the expression of this material plane energy is not manifest as one great and awful being to be feared and in that hysteria, actually revered, there have been those of your brothers who have given their focus to this energy. Among them were Hitler, Mussolini, and Tojo along with a group of supporters close to them. Their defeat was the pivotal point in the capacity of the forces of materiality to resist the Plan and its unfolding of the Christ energy. It was a necessary struggle and was carried out on many levels.

Their defeat at the end of what is known as the two world wars marked a turn toward the harmony, which comes through conflict. It was not only the breakpoint for the forces of materiality but also marked the coming of age of mankind in that you saw for the first time from a global and race perspective. Just as the seed thoughts of that war, indeed all wars, rested in the ideas of separativeness expressed as racial differences, the capacity of the race of humankind to conceptualize itself as a global-based race was given impetus and dramatically broadened. Thus, the very thing, the very goal and effort to fragment with fear and conflict set the world stage for its opposite, harmony. And while that harmony is not yet evident to most, its flowering in your time was set, framed and accelerated by the triumph of light and love over darkness.

For example . . .

The cooperation among brother nations with the beginnings of true sharing is now evident. International organizations whose purpose is to provide for this very sharing and cooperation are now many. Though the antecedents of these organizations were there before the war(s) of the century now past, they were given impetus by the two periods of conflict which you call WWI and WWII. There was, in reality, only one war.

The original League of Nations with its descendant organizations is another example.

But there is still anger, violence, persecution, neglect, war, murder, etc. in the world.

> Fear and its manifestations of separation and polarization are still evident and will be until you make the necessary changes. However, the capacity to make such change, indeed to even conceptualize that it can be and should be done, is now in the possession of the race and grows daily. The awareness that it is your responsibility is now possible and is the next great point of knowing in the awakening. This is coming to more and more of you each day. It is an idea whose time has come. It will come just in time. It will come with the help of the Masters.
>
> Also, the forces of materiality were not eliminated. Their function of upholding matter is necessary. Their desire to control through material things has not been broken. For them these lessons are yet to be learned and will be as their own process of evolution unfolds. Thus, there remains for a time yet, this negative energy. But, its days are numbered and it grows weaker each day. The retreat of these forces is in proportion to mankind's awakening and your invocation to "Let the Plan of Love and Light work out and may it seal the door where evil dwells."[19] The power of invocation on a racial/global scale is infinitely greater than that of any negative energy.

After a lifetime of learning to see evil as a real and vile something else to be hated, it is not easy to move to thinking of it as somehow part of everything.

Actually it has been many lifetimes and this is one of the reasons for the relative power of the negative energy. The conceptualizing by the race that such exists and has power is the basis for much of the power. Conversely then, a fundamental change in this fear-based consciousness has contributed to the condition whereby the decline of the power of the negative energy has come about.

As for the vile something else to be hated, remember the Unity principle. In all the manifested and unmanifested Universe there is only One thing. This One thing contains an infinite continuum of consciousness differentiated into distinct points of awareness. Each of these points of awareness has specific identity which is achieved at some juncture in the evolutionary process and which grows into ever greater awareness and consciousness of itself and in so doing takes on progressively the characteristics of the Creator. Once attained, this identity is never lost. The path of consciousness development is varied and, as contained within the Plan, is progressively influenced by the free will. This is true for your individual path as well as all others.

You say that these negative forces are still around?

Their influence may be seen where there is separation, especially on a large scale. Following the two world wars you saw the negative forces move to energize the cold war. While that conflict was characterized more by a standoff than world scale engagement, it was still conflict. It was still based upon fear and separation as well as the desire to dominate, control and profit. This pertained until recently when that situation, too, gave way to mankind's progress toward awakening. The end of the cold war marked another defeat of the negative energy and a new plateau in the consciousness of the race. It also marked another opportunity for mankind to demonstrate free will and to choose again even higher pathways of unity and brotherhood.

More recently you have seen the negative forces energize the current economic system which is based on competition, which is yet another form of fear-based separation, and the result is conflict. The so-called market economy has at its base fear of lack and loss. This, despite the observable fact that you live in an abundant world, which even now has enough of everything to meet all needs of everyone. Yet, every year millions die of preventable starvation, exposure and disease, most of them children. This grows worse each day as those with much more than they need continue out of fear to accumulate more at the expense of others who have less and less. As noted, it is this fear and resulting perception of separation that is at the root of the environmental crisis, which now threatens the continuation of your physical existence.

However, let us return to the larger picture. There is great hope, for mankind has arrived at the very threshold of the needed changes just in time to make them, and the pain of the continued conflict is positioning you to choose again and the will, free will, to choose harmony grows within the race on a global scale. It is this capacity that has allowed the Masters, that has given Them the wherewithal to move more directly to help, lead, and love you into the new dispensation where harmony may replace the conflict and sharing and cooperation will become revealed as the human norms that they are. As noted, it is not required that harmony come only through conflict. It may come also through an attitude of good will and a volitional posturing of loving kindness which naturally leads to sharing and cooperation.

Should we fear them at a personal level? Can they attack us and hurt us?

You should not fear anything. Nothing, no thing, can actually hurt you. However, there are some practical limits set by the law that may help you to see that conflict between forces have limits. One is that you will not ever meet a thing that appears as threat that you are not able to deal with. Thus, forces of darkness that may seem superior to you in strength may not engage you. You will get to deal with those that are at a level of your capacity. You get to deal with them as another opportunity to learn and grow in your understanding of reality; the reality of the Unity of all things.

You will be challenged by dark forces with fear. It is the only real weapon they have. So, look again for opportunities to see the fear and to heal it with the love energy of the Christ.

In this regard the Masters have a protective role in that They can and do shield you, the race, from undue influence by those who are more developed and who, for now, would see in their own separative view, you as opposed to their interests. This the Masters do within the law.

Lest we reinforce the very fear we are attempting to expose as false, let us quickly add that while there are individualized points that are more developed than you, there are none in the Earth energy field who are more developed than the Masters. The dark forces meet their match in Them. This is a great service that the Masters do for all of Their younger brothers and sisters.

It must also be noted that the fundamental change in the fear base of consciousness is being affected by many forces and that among them is the change of the environment of energy surrounding and flowing into the Earth.

How is there a change in the environment of energy surrounding and flowing into the Earth?

We have often said here that all is energy and there is nothing but energy. Thus, the physical Earth is an energy field set within a greater energy field which in turn is set within a greater energy field. It is reflective of the infinite continuum of consciousness differentiated into distinct points of awareness.

The greater field of energy, within which the Earth is evolving, is characterized by a great host of forces. These, too, are changing in their nature and intensity. Generally, they grow stronger and more refined and are more of the higher energy. This matches both the need for mankind to grow on its path and the capacity of mankind to grow, that is readiness, into higher levels of conscious awareness. These energies are in many forms. Included are those associated with the movement of the Earth into different alignment with the celestial bodies called constellations. This is an observable physical phenomenon and relates to the larger orbital path of the entire solar system. Additionally, there are other energies being directed from specific points and types of energy which are of the unfolding of the Plan on Earth. These include those noted before—the Lords of karma and those of the ray energies.

About ray energies, please understand that, consistent with that noted here several times, all is energy there is naught but energy. Rays of energy are being now poured into the Earth field of energy from many sources. These rays color and define the type and intent of such fundamental characteristics of the Plan as the Will, Love—Wisdom, and Active Intelligence of the Creator and they inform the evolution of each subunit of consciousness including that of each Soul in incarnation.

One's ray structure is the energy set established by the Soul for each experience in matter. Each of the seven ray elements carries a defined orientation of concepts such as mental and astral or emotional energy. These condition the way one's vehicles relate to, process, and integrate the energies of a particular life. Ray energy manifests on the material plane in association with the seven colors of the light spectrum.

Other great entities are also lending Their energy of love, will to good, and synthesis to the field at this time. All things work together for the greater good.

Correspondence is also reflected in the lower phenomena you call astrology which has its higher correspondent in a vast field of knowledge and wisdom dealing with the relationship of energies, including those of the planets and constellations within the context of their field of energy and how it interacts with all others including the individual lives of people, planets, and galaxies. This is another example of the law of correspondence—as above, so below.

We have touched on ray structure and now ray energy. Is there correspondence with the seven energy centers running up and down the spine called chakras?

Chakras are the major energy centers of the body. There are seven chakras spaced from the bottom of the spine to the top of the head. Each corresponds to a color of the visible light spectrum. These energy centers receive energy from the surrounding environment, move energy through the dense physical body and the other bodies or vehicles. They also radiate energy to the world of matter and so to other people. The latter point is especially true, at this time, of emotional energy.

You have been able to touch and sense a glimpse of the workings of chakras and their interplay with the Soul energy as that energy permeates the vehicles. The rendering which you labeled *Crowned Chakras*, may be of value to some who encounter this work and may serve as a visual concept.

The topics of rays and chakras are important. As there is already much on both that is available to the serious student, we will not put more effort into their study in this work preferring to stay with our larger intent of showing connections among broader concepts and the ubiquity of this connectedness. This, too, is an element of the law of correspondence which is a vast concept covering a dynamic natural law.

What then is the law of correspondence?

The greater truths and reality of the higher are reflected below in the form of ideas, which are in the process of evolving back to that greater reality. As first sensed or glimpsed and filtered through the little ego, this greater truth is often expressed by the little ego in a manner which is inside out, upside down, and backward, or at least incomplete. As higher consciousness evolves, the correct understanding of the concept also evolves.

Can You give a couple more examples?

An example would be a theory which is now of the lower but which reflects the higher. Such is that which is expressive of the higher reality of the unity of the one Sonship and is moving in awareness from the theory of the single Son to the single Sonship reality. You are all Sons and form together the Sonship and constitute a Oneness in the One Father.

Another example is that of the little ego conceptualizing itself as center of the Universe. This is reflective of the higher reality that the Soul is one with the Universe. Here the little ego still has it inside out and would settle for being only the center of the Universe. The reality is that with consciousness of connection to higher levels, you become aware that you are one with, and thus, the entire Universe. So, why would you want to be only the center when you could be the whole?

A further lesson in the little ego's inside out, upside down and backward concepts may be found in the current understanding that the traditional commandments are absolutes handed down by the proverbial angry, vengeful Father. The commandments are understood within this light as to be the opposite of what they really are. That is that they are actually prophecy given by a God of love who knows that all of His children will come home to and through the understanding that they love Him so that they love one another. Try reframing your view of these commandments and view them with new eyes that see them as statements of positive outcomes awaiting all as you grow.

This most certainly includes "A new commandment I give unto you, that you love one another . . ."[20] This, the core message of He who gave it, is actually a new dispensation that bears great moment and long study. It is nothing less than a sweeping away and negating of the old ways of fear and all separative thinking that went before. It thus becomes the way of knowing for each member of the Sonship and its Oneness, for He also told you that you would be known, that is, could gauge your own progress by your love for one another.

When understood, these simple words are world changing.

EXERCISE 6

PONDER ON THIS

Think on this deeply for several moments—NOW.

Imagine the implications of a world where each loved all and each as true brother and sister.

Return to this pondering over and over again as its understanding and implications blossom in your consciousness. Come to have this thought held in your heart from breath to breath.

PART EIGHTEEN

THE EGO AND COINCIDENCE NOT

Why the little ego in the first place?

Inherent here also is the lesson of why the little ego is necessary for your evolution. It is a waypoint on the journey to the fully integrated personality. The point of the fully integrated personality is reached when connection with the higher is consistent, and service to the Plan has replaced the separative agendas and desires of the little ego, lower mind and body. The fully integrated personality is required for the Soul to finish the journey through matter for the fully integrated personality is integrated with the Soul, which knows only service. In the last stages of growth, the Soul grips the highly developed personality and the final integration with the Soul is accomplished in relatively short order. Thus, the little ego evolves into a progressively more and more complex and receptive unit, or personality. It receives help from the Soul and Masters as needed and as it can use until at a relatively advanced point of personality development, it is ready for integration with the Soul.

Recognize the little ego for the child that it is and do not make it an object for further separative fixation—yet another ego trap upon which the little ego can perseverate. It is capable of such and would use this focus as a separative wedge just as it uses any other.

Thus, also does the Soul contribute to the Spiritualizing of matter as it works through the grounding in matter, the material world, which is afforded through its vehicle, the integrated personality.

Please tell me about the streetlight phenomena I have noticed for many years. It most often occurs when I am not looking for it and takes the form of a streetlight going on or off as I approach it in my car. This has been happening for many years in many different places. At one point very recently, however, it occurred such that for several days, at least seven, when I arrived under a particular streetlight, if it was on when I arrived right under it, it would go off. If it was off, it would go on. Daylight or dark did not seem to matter.

As you have already intuited, it is a sign. A friendly gesture, it is reflective of your own growing energy field as all personal experience is a grounding in the awakening process. It is a way of the Universe speaking to you, of reminding you, that we are all here and are all One. It is a way of suggesting that you focus on the higher when you are not so focused. The analogy of light and dark has not been lost on you and you are being reminded again, in a way that you find both interesting and filled with loving humor, to look up and in the metaphorical sense, to lighten up. The latter, to lighten up, is also meant at many levels and your thinking through its implications is a good learning process for you.

At least one point of knowledge about the lights going on and off was a wonderful reminder of my connection to all things. At one point I could literally feel this Oneness. It was so real to me as to register in my bones and cells. Thank You. It was of pure joy such that I wanted to share it with any who might be near.

The impetus to share received or newly arrived at awareness of the joy of inspiration and love in a spontaneous and gleefully communal way is one of the mechanisms of Creation and is hard wired in each Soul by the Creator. It is receiving and giving again. It is having the vessel filled and then experiencing the sheer bliss of emptying that vessel of its joy, to and with others so that it, the vessel, may be filled again and so that others may share by receiving, having their own vessel filled and thus able to perpetuate the cycle of joy by giving. It is the law of cycles, of giving and receiving, etc. It is loaves and fishes.

I also would like to know of any further significance and especially of the "village" as over a short period of only a few days I heard this term used many times within many contexts by many people. I came to understand that the sheer number of repetitions, like the streetlights, was out of the ordinary and meant for me to be cognizant of it. Also, when I would ask others about their use of the term, I received very interesting comments all related to the concept of village as metaphor for the entire human family.

Be prepared to see the unfolding of these phenomena of connection and moments of synchronicity. It is happening all over the material plane at this time and is of many levels of meaning and purpose. Among them are the Masters placing such events to get your attention to the existence of higher realms. It is also the natural flow of the connection of all things to all things being expressed on the material plane as thoughts arrived at by many of you in what appears to be independent thought processes coming to express similar things at the same time. There is much for the race to learn from these things that are now most often written off as only a curious and unscientific thing you call coincidence.

Many teachers of the higher Spiritual work instruct their students to begin a serious recognition of these happenings. As one begins to be aware of them they, over time, can tell you much and be events of light on your path. It is within this context that it is said that there are no accidents.

Be prepared to see this more and more as the Universe seeks your attention to the task at hand. That being nothing less than the next major unfolding of the knowledge and understanding of the race as it relates to your Spiritual Beingness. Think of moments of synchronicity as footsteps to God and join them and those who see them in recognizing them and taking joy in their signaling of things of the higher. Let each learn and appreciate as they are ready to see and see fit.

It seems that now that I have begun to register the synchronicity phenomena, it is more and more prominent.

> When something in this way does not manifest often, that is more notable than it manifesting.

I am wondering if some of my intuited meanings are correct. For example, in traffic I saw a sign that read in part—4U2C. My sense was that it could be read in two ways, "you to see" or "you, too, see" and that it was connected with our conversation about each of us having a Master and being able to "see" or otherwise know of that Master. In short order, I next saw a sign that had three letters at the beginning—EXP. This I saw as "expect"—meaning "expect to see a Master".

> You should continue to expect evidence of your own Master and also the physical appearance of the Master of the Masters Himself. He is emerging as you know and as we have talked of in these pages. The expectation of those who have this knowledge is a form of invocation. These two events were also personal for you. All such messages have many levels and one of the fun ways that a student comes to this kind of knowledge is through such lessons which contain not only the observation of a physical phenomenon but also the download of the intuitional experience. This is what happened to you. It was practice. It was information you can now process, use and share. In this case, you correctly intuit that it does also mean that you will see him and other Masters yourself and in a form appropriate to you, including physical form.

This will come in its time and accordance with the wisdom of your own Master.

You have also continued to experience the light phenomena. Expect this to continue and to be expressed in more ways than just the streetlights. Look for other light phenomena from all points that emit light on the material plane. Also, expect to see light in places and in ways that are not of your traditional and still narrow understanding of the material plane. This light phenomena which you continue to note, should bring joy. You are continued in the admonishment to lighten up. This should be taken in all of its meanings.

You have the capacity to bring light and it is your joy to do so. Do so. Remember, it is your birthright to have joy. Remember also, that which you share, you strengthen. That which you teach, you learn. Share light and teach joy. All else will be added unto you.

Let this be a service that you consciously render. It will be the next step in your learning to consciously focus and shine your light into the mind of your brother. As noted in <u>A Course In Miracles</u>, your mind, each of your minds, is such a light unto each other. You have the capacity to enlighten the mind and the path of your brother. Each of you must learn that your mind is a very powerful thing. Its light can literally reach into the mind of your brother and enlighten his mind. In so doing, you affect his awakening, healing and atonement. This is also true of a Master relative to your own mind and is done because They too, as you, are the same mind, the Christ mind, the very mind of God.

Indeed, the perfect match for the learning you need is the teacher who is your brother, whether you are sending or accepting this light, it is like unto the giving and receiving, which are both one in the same. Either way, light is shared and thus strengthened and lessons are taught and thus learned and so does the Sonship grow and expand in awareness and energy.

We have again referenced Masters. Some more please on the origins and current whereabouts of the Masters.

They have been here since taking Their first life and have evolved through all of the roles of mankind's many and varied experiences. They were originally assisted in Their growth by higher beings whom They have now replaced. They are the first born in the sense that among Them are the first to move to and through the first five initiations. It is the decision of Those who form the Hierarchy of this planet to remain with you and to serve the Plan of evolution for Earth. Their own growth thus continues in this service with many of Them having surpassed the fifth initiation.

They work as an intelligent group. They look with love for leadership, guidance, and inspiration to the great Lord, who is senior among Them, the Master of the Masters. They all work under the direction of the Lord of the World and They serve the Plan.

Historically, They have stood behind the workings of the race from its early days and influenced directly events and the evolution of the race toward growth in ever higher levels of consciousness. In earlier times this was done by physical presence and actually walking among you. The period of this direct physical contact was deliberately ended some 20,000 years ago at which time the Masters withdrew into remote areas of the Earth from which They continued Their work.

Their work has been done through influencing world leaders and thinkers. Ever bound by the law, They can only show receptive persons the higher ideas and ways. Those who are at a point of receptivity to such impression receive suggestions through dreams, inspirations, intuitive flashes, visions, messengers, and occasionally through personal visits. The individual so impressed may or may not remember the moment of contact or its vehicle. He or she may simply awaken from a nap or a night's sleep with the solution to the problem at hand or a new insight into the next steps of a process. They are free to accept or reject this impression.

A major way of influencing the Spiritual growth has been the sending into the world of a high initiate to act as messenger and teacher. This has been done whenever it was needed and corresponds to periods of crisis and transition. Many, many have been so sent, indeed there has never been a time when there were not any such among you. You tend to recognize and remember the major ones who have come at roughly 2000-year intervals. Among Them were Gautama, Jesus and Mohammed. And, while these methods will continue to be used as needed, the new phase of work now coming to fruition will allow the Masters to move openly among you and to be heard and seen in a physical body again.

As for where They are, They have never not been here. Their withdrawal into more remote locations was not a departure from a physical presence on the Earth. The remote locations included small communities in the deserts and mountains of the world such as the Himalayas and Gobi Desert. From these places They continued to anchor Their physical forms and to do the work of Hierarchy: Their work in bringing the Plan of God to fruition.

This withdrawal has now allowed for the necessary unfolding of energies and needed developments of the race so that once again They are able to go out among you and will be more effective in this direct way. This They are doing by moving from the more remote places to position Themselves in strategic places, which generally correspond to the major energy centers on the planet. These are, in most instances, large cities. Here, They are taking up residence and preparing for the next phase of Their emergence into your awareness and consciousness. Remember, this must be done under law and without infringement of the free will.

What cities?

Places like London, Rome, New York, Tokyo, Darjeeling, and other major cities in every area of the world.

They are thus positioned to gradually but progressively move into the society of each of these major centers and to expand your awareness of Them via an expansion of the frequency of Their physical presence in these places. However, They are not limited to these places and may appear anywhere on the Earth as They see need in Their work of serving the Plan.

PART NINETEEN

PART-TO-WHOLE

May I please have more on Who and/or what You are—
my Holy Spirit?

An outpost of the consciousness of God Himself:
In order to understand this you must try and
comprehend something, which at this point is
literally incomprehensible to you. And that is the
true nature and extent of the Being that is God.
However, let us try because your natural curiosity
is a blessing and because man's reach truly should
ever exceed his grasp. Do keep in mind though
that we will be using lower order conceptualization
to define higher level realities and there will be a
fundamental point of tension around a dissonance,
which is unavoidable.

So toward a cosmology then: the Beingness that is
God is the Creator, superstructure, infrastructure,
content, past, present, future, planner, holder,
maintainer, macrocosm, microcosm and sum total
of the Universe, and the Universe of Universes, and
beyond. This is what we mean when we say God.
Some of the qualifying characteristics of this Being
include unconditional love, omnipresence, joy, light,

consciousness of and on an infinite continuum, awareness of each part of Itself, creativity, peace, laughter, bliss, patience, harmony, wholeness, inclusivity, evocation, service, wisdom, caring, compassion, omnipotence, truth, play, energy, intuition, evolution, and the spark of God—that individualized Soul that you and each of your brothers are/is, have always been and always will be.

Having said all that, you still do not have any grasp of that greater Being, Who enSouls this and all other Universes. By definition it is not possible at your level for the created to comprehend in the least the Creator. Thus, you are encouraged to focus on that highly advanced and, relative to your state, appropriately awesome, in the most loving sense of that term, Being Who is the One Who enSouls this Earth when you focus your attention on God, Mother, Father, Creator, Supreme Being, and in general Big Kahuna. Indeed, all of the foregoing descriptors apply to that Being. It is this Being Who is your true and most immediate, direct Creator. It is this Being Who demonstrates to you and through you, after all you are created in His image and are endowed with the potential and in the long view, imperative, to evolve the characteristics in the preceding listing.

At another level there is an infinitely more highly developed Being, the One so highly developed that It enSouls the galaxy, the only sense of Whom, at your stage of development, can be that It is somehow an aggregate of all lesser developed beings, there is nothing else you can really say and or understand. Therefore, in the literature of the Wisdom this

Being is known as and actually named: *The One About Whom Naught May Be Said*. It is not that you should not speak of this Being; it is that your ignorance is so profound and fundamental that, in reality, there is nothing you can say. Thus also, any discussion of that great *Beingness* above the galactic level is not appropriate for this work.

Returning then to the encouragement to focus on that highly advanced and, relative to your state, appropriately awesome, in the most loving sense of that term, Being who is the One Who enSouls this Earth let us first point out that God's awareness is total totality. This includes the ability to have awareness and intellectual focus as you have, on any object or thought that you choose to put your attention upon and into. The difference is that God can do this for every aspect of all of Creation all at once. Thus, a fragment of God's consciousness, an outpost of that consciousness, forms the Holy Spirit. As such, I, the Holy Spirit, am in communion with the greater Being that is God. This communion is constant and complete always and in all ways. Therefore, I Am He Who sent Me unto you.

Therefore, to say what or who is the Holy Spirit, you must first understand that this awesome Beingness has the capacity to have continuity of consciousness of each part of Its Being all the time. Thus, it is truly said that a sparrow ". . . shall not fall on the ground without your Father."[21]

It is also truly said that you cannot separate yourself from your Creator. This is because you are literally of Him who created you as He did so by sharing His Being with you. It is this that is the source of your power. This power is real. This power is limitless. The coming to awareness of this reality, *The Reality* of the Unity of all things in God, is your great gift and opportunity. It is why you are. It is unto and into this gift which you and your brothers are awakening.

I have tried to avoid a constant stream of comments that show my astonishment. This however must be said— wow!

There is more. Do you want to continue with this line of revelation?

Does the Pope have kneepads?

We understand that to be an affirmative. Very well, by extrapolation you, too, are God and, within the context of developing through evolution, are gods in the making. The small "g" here would refer to the point in the infinite continuum of consciousness differentiated into distinct points of awareness, at which you are.

This is a simple extrapolation that is often hard for those just beginning to awaken to grasp. If you are part of a thing, you are that thing. This goes back to the ability of the little ego to separate you in its little thought from the greater whole, which you are. Indeed this is one way of defining the little ego. It would have you believe that even parts of your physical self are not you and thus uses this inside out and upside down reasoning as analogy to convince you that, you are not of and intrinsically exist as the greater Thing which is God—The One in Whom you live and move and have your being.

Thus, too, are Masters, your elder brothers, Beings who have gone before and know more of the Plan and the path and have developed Their own capacity for consciousness to a much, much greater level than your present capacity. Their consciousness is such They have the ability to have awareness and intellectual focus as you have on any object or thought that you choose to put your mental awareness upon and into. The difference is that a Master can do this for aspects of all the Earth and its cosmic environs all at once. This means awareness of you and Their other brothers. This is true of all the Masters and especially the One that They look to as their own Master. As already noted, this is One, who embodies the very energy of the Christ and who has taken the Spiritual name Maitreya.

Let us also note again that Master within this context does not mean the more traditional use of the term as the ego would project it and fear it, that of driver, overlord, and dominator. It carries a higher definition that indicates One who has Himself Mastered the lower worlds, particularly that of the material, and understands through hard experience the meaning of unconditional Love and who is positioned to gladly share that meaning and teach, guide, and mentor His younger brothers.

EXERCISE 7

PART-TO-WHOLE RECOGNITION

See the nail on one of your fingers. What part of it is not of the finger? What part of the finger is not of the hand? What part of the hand is not of the arm? What part of the arm is not of the body?

Stand in front of a mirror and ask yourself the question: What part of what I see is not me? Ask this question incrementally and situationally of things and especially your brothers as you encounter them throughout the day. See in your mind all of humanity standing together in brotherhood and ask what part of us is not mankind.

Next visualize the picture of the planet from space. Ask: What part of this picture is not Earth? Then think of yourself standing under a starry sky and think of the body out from which you look, the near landscape, the distant objects and the horizon where the canopy of stars begins. Ask the questions: What part of what I see is not the Universe? What part of what I see is not God?

If it is God in the aggregate, then it is God in each of Its parts. The success of the illusion maintained by the little ego depends entirely upon your continuing not to see this simple connection—you are a part of God and, therefore, are of God and, therefore, are God and in the case of final reference, more specifically to the sojourn in materiality, God in the making by being God in the learning. As soon as you see this, the little ego's days are numbered for it is at that point you have begun to pierce the veil of illusion of specialness and to see that the emperor has no clothes.

EXERCISE 8

WOVEN ONENESS

high speed slow motion,
in-flight aircraft assembly,
energized fatigue,
precise vagueness,
peaceful disturbance,
stormy tranquility,
instantaneous timelessness,
disheveled order,
noisy silence,
blessed disaster,
chaotic stillness,
irrelevant imperative,
finite uncertainty,
monolithic gestalt,
holographic singularity,
isolated unity,
holy whole!

While we are onto definitions, please define the little ego in terms of consciousness.

> The little ego is a fragment of your own mind. It has consciousness but that consciousness is incomplete and it has mistaken a partial level of awareness for all that there is. The little ego defines the Universe in terms of itself as opposed to defining itself in terms of the Universe. It is the example of whole-to-part confusion as it refuses delivery of the message that there is a whole unto which it belongs. It is a sliver of your own consciousness, which has taken unto itself the whole, the all.
>
> The little ego does not wish the greater you, the reality that you are awakening into, to have an awareness of the journey and that journey's potential. It fears the greater you, the integrated and integrating personality, because it knows that your growing awareness means the end of its ability to keep you glamoured, enthralled, and afraid and thus circumscribed by its littleness: that very same littleness, which it defines as the Universe.
>
> In order to define itself, this fragment of your mind partners with the body and other little egos, none of which it trusts or wishes well but instead relates to in a usurious way. The partnering is done in order to effect a solidification of control and the level of denial necessary by the little ego and all others in order to insulate first itself, and then the greater you, from the reality of the still greater you, the Soul.

Thus, the little ego is the example of wrong relationship. It is exclusive and not inclusive. It desires to perpetuate ignorance and error. It is the center of the Universe. It is inside out, upside down, and backward. It is afraid and angry and thoroughly pitiful. It is the last thing to which you should hand the keys to the Kingdom.

By analogy the Holy Spirit is an outpost of the consciousness of God; a Master is a major endowed consciousness of God up from the human evolution and the little ego is a dot of your Soul's consciousness.

While we are defining here, would You please address the greater you?

Yes. The greater you is that part, note here part not whole, which is the progressively integrating personality. It is that part on its way to becoming integrated with and through the larger part(s) of your mind. This process usually takes many, many lifetimes as one first permits the construction of the little ego, a necessary step, and then must subordinate this creation to the ever-unfolding larger self. The greater you is the Soul in its becoming.

You used Soul as a counterpoint in defining the little ego. How do we define the Soul?

The Soul is a vast point of consciousness which has conceptualized the greater you and is in the process of using that greater you as, in effect, an intelligent probe on the material plane in order to learn the lessons of the material plane and at the same time to Spiritualize matter. In so doing, it is hastening the development of the integrated personality. The truly integrated personality is so by virtue of its being integrated with the Soul and aware at the personality level of the integration. Thus, it on its own level of function as you on yours, is effecting the unfolding of the Plan. The Soul needs you, including the physical, emotional, and mental bodies, to accomplish this. It needs your awakening, connection, awareness and coming into your own Beingness.

The Soul relates to you as instrument of its own creation and as you grow in your awareness you relate to the Soul as yourself. Indeed you are the Soul. Any form of the higher work, the threshold to which the race has now come, will require not just the recognition but the understanding and assimilation into the knowledge that you are the Soul. This is one of the most fundamental of all lessons of the Wisdom at this time.

And of that golden rule?

As above, so below: The golden rule has in its axiomatic and mantra-like aspects, great value as a guide for striving toward brotherhood. However, as above so below, it also is revelatory of a higher truth and actual function in that it is a description of what is the reality of what happens when you meet a brother. Each such meeting is a holy encounter in which you really and truly are doing unto others as you would/will have done unto you. For you cannot really meet another, you meet only a being who, like you, is a part of the greater being that you all are, a part of God, and as such is your very self. And in that holy meeting are you able to recognize and be mutually healed by the Divinity that you jointly are. Thus is it also truly said that where two or more are gathered together, there I Am also.

So, at the level above striving to treat your neighbor as yourself is a truth that you cannot help but embody. In each moment you do so because (remember the law of aggregation) your brother, just as you, is a part of all and has within that same spark of the Divine. Hence, your interaction with your brother in thought, word or deed is an interaction with a part which, like you, is the whole. You are then, literally, interacting with another of the same mind. Thus, it has been truly said, "We have met the enemy and he is us."[22]

Therefore, when you think of your neighbor in any way you are reflecting but how you think of yourself. This includes all thoughts of blessing, love, joy, fear, anger, and hate. In so doing, you create the very thought-form, a real and tangible thing, of the conceptualization you have made which at the same instant goes out to your brother and into you. Remember that giving is receiving and that what you see is what you get. Thus, the way to keep something, including blessing, love, joy, fear, anger, and hate, is to give it away.

EXERCISE 9

SEE ALL AND BLESS ALL

Standing with arms outstretched, embrace all the Earth and each individuated point of energy and point of light upon it.

See within your out-stretched arms that you are holding a sphere. That sphere is as large as the room in which you are or the street upon which you stand or the forest within which you imagine yourself to be. Within that sphere see all life as blessed and visualize all of that life as flowing with the golden light of love and healing. Recognizing that to heal is to make whole, bless all with the light of love and healing and know that you are part of what you see, love, and heal.

Then visualize a ball as tall as your own head—a giant beach ball. Within it concentrically are an infinite number of such spheres. You are holding this one as your Master is holding the one which contains you, and as God is holding the one containing your Master. You and your becoming are thus blessed, whole and holy.

PART TWENTY

THE WORK

Holy Spirit, getting away from this journal for several weeks that included a few days of holiday, I once again sit to write and realize that the connection I seek, repeatedly ask for and whine about has been, but for only a few moments, totally gone and not even missed.

Where have I been?

> A period of distraction by the lower as well as a period of settling and processing. All is governed by cycles. You have/are in such.

There have been so many times, not just these last few weeks but daily, when I simply do not feel the same call to write?

> It is part of your growth. It is an adjustment to the new way of thinking and processing. You have chosen this and may choose again.
>
> Ask and ye shall receive. Of late you have been asking more. Also, you must listen. It is your choice to listen or not. You have often been distracted.

The lower is still strong and the first to get your attention.

I grow impatient at the time I am not able to connect. However, that is often in hindsight.

You will have what you want. As you were told—you have come far. Recognize this. It is also good to ask where to go next. This is what you are doing now.

EXERCISE 10

*AN ENERGY MOVEMENT AND HEALING
VISUALIZATION FOR WHEN YOU ARE
READY TO SEE AND THEREBY ASSIST
YOUR BROTHER OR SISTER TO SEE
THAT THE TWO OF YOU ARE SELF, ONE
WITH EACH OTHER AND ONE WITH ALL*

Either in the presence of him and with or without his brain level knowledge and/or through the use of the creative imagination, see your brother standing a few arms lengths in front of you facing you with you also standing. See a tube of golden light emanating from the right side of your chest, at the level of your heart center and flowing to your brother in a curve that takes it into his heart center on his left side. See the tube of light after passing through his heart center, emanating from his right side and flowing to you in a curve that takes it into your heart center on your left side and after passing through your heart center from whence it originally sprang as you initiated it, back to him, thus completing a circle and circuit.

Allow this to continue for a few moments as you open to the concept that giving is receiving, that healing is being made whole in each other, and that the healer does not do something to the one being healed but receives so as to give again.

You may vary the color of the light and focus it on any center, or with practice use this with all centers and their respective color either one at a time or simultaneously. But always it goes and comes in the way at the same intensity as you projected it, as you intended it. Thus, as you heal (make whole and holy) your brother, you make whole and holy and heal yourself.

It is the same energy that you share because it is the same mind you are—the mind of God. This then is the significance of the term "The One in Whom we live and move and have our Being."

The pace and fatigue of daily events and my outer work are a problem. Can You help me here?

But of course! I can help you anywhere.

Lighten up. Be a light.

As you continue to view the world of work as outer and, as used by you here, separate from your inner work you will continue to have the burden of maintaining the ego structures of that perceived separation. This requires ever greater amounts of energy as your growing awareness of things of the higher call you to let go of the sense of separation as real.

You are where you need to be. Others have already been sent to you. See this as proof. Your direction should be seen as reinforcing.

When do I get to bliss and fun while staying balanced, connected and aware of and in the higher work?

Soon, very soon.

Often, I am just too tired to get up at 3:30 a.m. and go to the computer.

You need balance. We have talked of this before. Look to the three lower bodies for balance in body, emotions and mind. Also, remember, too, that this is a time of turmoil like no other. Your need for balance is actually ongoing and at times, soon to be discovered by you, a minute-by-minute need to assess and correct at the level of thought, word, and deed. This will include an awareness of what you eat and drink and how you give appropriate attention to maintenance of these lower instruments. This will be necessary for the time it takes to use them as the growth mediums that they are. In time they will be seen from the higher as illusory and you will be able to move away from their now seeming imperatives including the sense of fatigue.

Okay, but also the sense of a strong feeling of knowing, that intuitive—ah-hah, is not evident as it once was.

Partly glamour, partly lack of focus but also, as we have noted here before, you grow more accustomed to the new energy that you are receiving and learning to wield.

Also, you are hearing more and better as you wish. Keep up the practice. It will not always be a direct voice. This is so that you will learn to hold your own counsel and to think and know for yourself, even though all is connected. In this way you grow into a point of light on your own and begin to take your place as a disciple who has his own work and core of knowing. You have learned much and have much to share when, in your evolving wisdom, you know that the circumstance is right.

Lighten up. Laugh and encourage laughter as you did yesterday. Share joy. It is yours to have and you already know that to keep it, you must give it away.

Have confidence that you now know things in your own right. Have faith in your own ability to come forward with the Truth and manifest it. Know that you have grown to a point of developing the beginnings of autonomy so necessary to moving forward with the work.

Detachment is the way for you now. Humor, laughter are ways of detaching.

I seek to move myself forward so as to detach. I also see my own efforts compared to those who suffer so much as small and less worthy of my time and Yours.

Setting of priorities is ever the task of the disciple and involves a vision of your part of the Plan. Your effort is really directed to seeking that, which will give you the clarity.

And this comes from Soul contact?

It does.

Is there a mechanism or technique that will allow me to know, have a more direct sense, when and how that act of Soul communication is happening and can be enhanced?

Seek to focus in the moment, the eternal now. You have been able to do this some of late. You are closer than you think.

Where do we go next?

To heaven: to a place where you already are.

What do I do next?

It is not so much what to do as to be. In the moment, be in that moment. Be that moment.

Continue to teach this so as to learn it.

On a more personal note, while on the recent trip which took me away from this journal and away from my sense of connecting, I experienced a several hour drive on the interstate in Florida. I saw the number two come into my field of view over and over and over again. It was on the license plates of cars, on road sign after road sign, on billboards, in pairings of birds and airplanes, and on the odometer of the car I was driving. Not just a single and random occurrence but multiple instances of multiple appearances of the number two appearing multiple times. I called it a torrent of twos.

> All notes are both personal and at some level reflective of the greater whole. Indeed, this journal is an example of just such.

> This was more evidence of your unfoldment and enfoldment. You were and are sent many messages, all the time. As noted in this narrative the Universe is, I am, singing to you and with you all the time. These times when you become aware of it are periods of relatively greater awareness than others. It is the very connection that you have missed at times being manifest. It is the now. It is the moment to get into in preparation for being in and Being.

> It is also significant as a message for you to keep light and to lighten up. How did you feel when you began to recognize this happening?

I was at first curious and then found it fascinating. Later as I tried to surrender to it, I found it funny and fun. I laughed out loud and said "Okay, you have my attention."

I then asked what does it mean and heard it was about healing soon to come.

> The joy in the experience was natural. It is your birthright to have this joy. Also, the numbers were to tell and foretell of the near coming to fruition of events hoped for and long ago sown.

I ask again to hear Your voice all the time, to be able to connect and stay connected.

> Thank you: A worthy goal.

> This you already have. Continue to train yourself to listen.

Is there a key or trigger that I could use to help me get and stay in the listening, the communion? Or, am I asking again for the 800 number?

> You are asking again and it is good to ask. From asking comes the next new beginning and step which is also the next awareness of the return to what you already know, of remembering who and what you are.

> This you have referenced several times and returned many times to the issue of the 800 number, connectedness, magic bullet, etc., and how to get and stay there. You have even called it your Spiritual whining. It is important to acknowledge that there is a higher correspondent at work here. It is in all of you. Remember that any reference to the you, the little ego that is yours, the student who thinks he is scribing this narrative, is

intended and is in reality a plural "you" meant for all of you—your brothers and sisters.

The higher correspondent is the built-in need for a return to the awareness of that which you never left. It is the imperative to rediscover the knowing, the knowingness that the connecting means. It is the call of the higher that, once heard, may not be denied. It may be avoided for many lives in the many ways that the little ego is susceptible to and capable of. However, it, the celestial call, may never be unheard. It may not be undone. So, you have many times returned to the questions of the connection and will do so again and again until the approximations that flow in the form of answers from each holy question lead inevitably to centeredness in the understanding you seek. It is in the Plan that you ask and ask and ask again. It is in your genes for it leads home to the peace that passes understanding. It leads to the awakening, the atonement, the sweet reunion: The known and understood oneness with the all that is, The One.

A memory device may help, however; the symphony is ongoing. To hear, you must only be still for a moment. Use your "OM." You have had practice with it.

A question I like to pose is, "So what?"

All this is to answer the "So what" question. It is to help you see and become functional during this time of great shift and to recognize this as a shift so profound as to allow you to alter the very way in which you think about what you think about.

It is the grand happening that allows you to claim your center in the name and of the essence of who you are, to be the love that you are and command it for all. No one said that you would want to go or even see the need to go into this new time. Yet all now cry out for it and must have this new growth into a new understanding or perish. It is their pain that you feel along with your own ego investment.

You are becoming. The experience is what helps you to become. All experience is ultimately that help and therefore neither good nor bad. To the extent that it is perceived as pain, it spurs action and a search. How you respond, how you choose to respond is the real experience therefore. It is the point of growth and not the happening itself. Any happening is a gift, an opportunity to move to learning. Your response is the act of that learning.

The neat thing is, the real gift is, that you may at any time rethink your response to any happening and/or choose a different response when next gifted by the same opportunity in the form of another happening. Thus, you will grow to see experience as the basis for the response of trying and learning. There is no experience then that is good or bad. And no response is good or bad even when you repeat it for lifetimes until you grow past it.

You are here to have such experience. It is the point of the physical world you have created.

Share this and make it real for all whom you meet. Teach it so that you may learn it.

Gandhi said "Be the change you want to see in the world."

That is the "So what."

EXERCISE 11

THE SO WHAT QUESTION

A mental discipline to build the thought-forms for the shift and beyond. Slowly read and repeat each phrase aloud. Look into how each builds on the other and allows you to arrive at a new way of thinking about what you think about:

First know that there is nothing but God, the One Creator. In all of Creation, both the manifest and the unmanifest, there is only One Thing.

The One Creator created all including you, out of an act of Love.

The Creator loves you because you exist and not because of anything you do, have done, or will do: Your pictures are on God's refrigerator.

You are a Spiritual being having a physical experience so that you may come to know the Creator's love on the level of the Creator's thought known to you as the material world and to own this love in and of yourself for you may not share in what you do not have.

You are having this physical experience so that you will come to love all others on this material plane as the Creator loves you and in so doing to Spiritualize matter and to truly understand the fuller meaning of "as above, so below."

PART TWENTY ONE

FORGIVENESS

When will the Master begin his outward work?

> He already has.

When will I/we see Him?

> You already have and will again. You do not want to hear the word "soon", but that is the best answer.
>
> Also, remember that it will not be Him doing and accomplishing some *fait accompli* but your responding to the new opportunity that is the real significance of His coming. You will have to act. He will not "do" it for you. Thus, you do not need to "wait" for His appearance. And this you know.
>
> Love all. Serve all.

You have many times referenced relative to the us that is me and all of my sisters and brothers, "the power"; what does it mean?

It is for you the next level and it has been a long time in coming. For this you have trained long and hard. It has and will come so that you may take the next steps. It is the unfolding of the power of your Master, the power of the Spirit, the power of the Universe and the One Itself. You are not so much being given It as you are awakening to It as all will in time.

I have come to a time of transition and am asking for guidance and assistance. I have a growing sense that it is time to seek a new beginning on some things but also sense a period of suspension or waiting while things are moved out of and into place. May I have some practical suggestions and guidance please?

You are always receiving guidance. Listen. It is becoming more easy with each awareness. You have seen it in practice now many times. Use it often and always. Serve the highest good and detach from the result. The result is not yours to craft in these early stages. That will come in its own time and wisdom. Your Master has this responsibility and the Power.

You have much support. You will have all the guidance and resources you need. As you yourself have said, the Universe is a just-in-time supplier. Look for and expect this to demonstrate and work out more and well for you. Share this with others who are ready to see and use it.

You have correctly surmised that this period of break is for rest as well as an opportunity to focus on closures and transitions. It is also good to acknowledge that there are things to come that you do not know, cannot foresee and must trust and have faith in. Remember, a Master always prefers what occurs. As do you. Welcome what is as it is for and *is* you. It is your very essence being manifest so that you may see it and experience it. The experiencing of it has come to be seen wrongly as separate from it. Greet and embrace each unfolding, in that which you still see as time, with new eyes of joy and wonder. It is a celestial play of the Plan and it is for your joy. It is of the Father and His gift. As you are of the Father and His gift to this play of the Plan and all who are in it with you, which is all of your brothers; every Father's Son of you.

Be blessed yourself and of good cheer. Has not the Master told you that all will be well? Trust that it will come to pass again for you as it has in the past.

Also, you have asked for help and have seen it come in the form of people who reflect your love back to you. They too need you and your wisdom for and of them. Seek them as needed. You were not meant to grow alone but with all others. There are those who would appear to be against this growth. You know this is not so. Let them go. Leave them to their Souls. You are all on the same team—the only team.

Even now, after our wonderful work and play on this journal together, I still find that there are times when I encounter a situation or more usually a brother who is so into the ego and its fear that I come away wondering how in this world, Lord, are we going to awaken in time to avoid the consequences of our currently fear-based thoughts, words, and deeds?

> You have come far in your understanding and those encounters you reference are now for you but opportunities to practice your harmlessness, nonjudgment, and forgiveness, and to enfold your brother in the love that will bring the atonement. Never doubt the capacity of Love to reach across any perceived distance. When such doubt comes, heal it in yourself first with love and then give that healing out to a world that is now screaming for it.

> We must soon close this narrative. Already here there are enough points for the student who so chooses to find many portals into further study.

You reference the need to bring this part of the work to a close. I can now see that. Are there things You would have us touch upon before we close?

> We have managed to cover a lot of things each in its own right worthy of many volumes. Indeed many volumes on each already exist if mankind would but seek them with open eyes and heart. Be reminded also, one of our major themes here is that there are many, many avenues, doors and windows. There are as many different steps on the path as there are people and while most still perceive themselves and their steps, or more pointedly for this analogy, the body of knowledge to which they relate as having the truth, in separatist terms there is no such thing as separation, for each body of knowledge contains kernels of truth and all are connected.

As you are fond of the oxymoron and have in the past articulated such as: jumbo shrimp, pretty ugly, and smart bomb, let me add another to your list: duality.

There remain at least three items that it would benefit many to be given the opportunity to have more focus upon. They include the concepts of judgment and forgiveness. Though already touched upon, these are of such importance that we need to visit them further. The third item is a question of great cosmic significance that I will pose to you at our end of this work.

Very well then, more focus on judgment please.

Judgment is error. It is seeing the brother or situation as separate. When you engage this you are setting the stage for a predictable and very old pattern to repeat. It repeats now at your peril. The old and wrong relationship pattern is launched when you first choose to judge and then make a fundamental judgment that your brother is separate from you and not of the whole and Holy Oneness that is the Unity of all things. Again, once this judgment is made, you then make either one of two further judgments, both false by definition because the context is one of exclusion flowing from the assumptive position of separativeness. The judgment is that your brother is inferior to you or superior to you.

In the case of your belief that he is inferior, you feel threatened either by your own projected fear of attack or that his fate may somehow befall you. You then feel that you can and should control this perceived threat, and with righteousness and impunity, allow, or visit directly by your own thought, word or deed, any manner of hostility, punishment, and pain upon him. The result is wrong relationship and whatever thought, word or deed that has resulted from your original judgment returns to you via the law of karma.

In the case of your belief that he is superior, you then feel threatened by your own projected fear of attack or that his fate may somehow not befall you. You then feel that you can and should control this perceived threat, and with righteousness and impunity, allow, or visit directly by your own thought, word or deed, any manner of hostility, punishment, and pain upon him. The result is wrong relationship and whatever thought, word or deed that has resulted from your original judgment returns to you via the law of karma.

The reason for the "I am superior/he is superior" thoughts in the first place is that you do not understand and accept your own worth as a created Son of the one Father. This is the littleness trap of the ego.

From a point of understanding and true internalizing of your own worth, you can see all others as they truly are—your equal. When you know yourself as sinless and worthy of God's love then you can see your brother in the same light. You may not give what you do not have.

When you find that you are disturbed by the actions of a brother or a situation, it is a signal, an opportunity to examine carefully first your own place, perspective, and reactions. Most of the time when you do this, if you would to thine own self be true, you will see that you are caught up in judgment and that this point of judgment but begins another ego cycle. It is just the latest of literally hundreds of thousands that have gone before and, unless you see it and change it, will be. Judgment is one of the most subtle of the ego's ways because it is so clearly correct in the upside down world rationale of the ego and thus so is its following logic of separative thinking.

Put others neither above you nor below you in any way for this results in a drain on your own energy to maintain either position. It does not, as you may delude yourself, come at any cost to those whom you judge to be in any way other than your peer, equal, and a true brother or sister. It is a burden of great cumulative weight and energy drain. It will put aches and trouble in your head, plaque in your veins, steal life from your living, and prolong your journey in the illusion. Only the little ego thinks of this as right. However, it is madness.

I tell you this, hear it clearly, the attempt to control through punishment, either in thought, word or deed that flows from judgment, is one of the most wrong minded of all of your separative thought-forms. Because it has become so prevalent and accepted as truth, this belief alone has led in large measure to the current state of woe and great danger.

However, there is another and, in the cosmic view, even more compelling reason to learn to recognize and begin to deal with judgment as the false thing that it is. It is not that you are threatened with the retribution of an angry God if you engage in judgment, for this your Father simply does not do. It is not even that you incur like energy through the law of karma, although within limits this is true. Instead you are being admonished to actively cultivate the capacity to give up judgment because at this point in your unfolding, it is simply beyond your capacity.

You do not know The Plan of God. You do not know the consequences of the actions of another on the working out of that brother's path in the greater Plan. In recognition of the fact that you are not yet equipped to judge, give your brother and yourself the gift of forgiveness. This will serve you both.

I judge that I have much to learn on this point.

There is humor in your response. It is a good thing. You are also correct that you and almost everyone alive on the Earth right now have much to learn on this point. That is why we needed to refocus on it now.

In that Spirit then, I am sorry I could not resist the pun, more focus please on forgiveness.

The Spirit is willing and pleased.

Forgiveness is a powerful tool I have brought you to deal with the error of judgment. It is a perfect match and when applied with honesty of mind, sincerity of Spirit and detachment will, I promise you, render judgment an impotent threat to be placed among all other false responses that you have learned.

Forgiveness will heal aches and trouble in your head, remove plaque from your veins, return life to your living, and shorten greatly your journey in the illusion. Forgiveness will also allow you to gift these things to your brother. It is sanity.

Forgiveness is the new dispensation that completely negates the old "eye for an eye." Thus you have been instructed to forgive not just seven times but ". . . seventy times seven."[23]

Forgiveness is not a passive acceptance. Action to resolve the fear(s) is needed. This, too, when done with love, is an act of forgiveness and will range from thought, word and/or deed and should be done with intent to establish and extend right relationship.

Forgiveness flows from the head and the heart, from the mind and Spirit. Forgiveness is both a learned feeling process and a learned thought process. Forgiveness is to be consciously practiced and eventually so learned that practice is no longer needed because it has become a pattern of first response and enduring response.

Forgiveness is a very broad and potent antidote to the fear of the little ego and the cascade of responses that flow from fear. Forgiveness works on many levels at the same time and all the time.

Forgiveness can be retroactive to any memory, any situation, and any persons living or what you still think of as dead. Forgiveness is a blanket of correction and awakening that you may spread over any place, time, event, thought or concept of any size.

Forgiveness is at its essence a capacity for deep, profound, liberating atonement and healing of both you and your brother. Forgiveness is self-generated miracle.

You must only do three things in order to move off of the battlefield of hurt, harm, and hate and onto the playground of love and joy: forgive, forgive, forgive. In the higher level of understanding of "to thine own self be true" forgive first yourself for judging that you are capable of judging, then, second, your brother for what he did not do, and third, the ego for perceiving itself as all there is. Then let go.

EXERCISE 12

HEALING THROUGH FORGIVENESS

Using your new clarity of vision, be alert and look for times of fear which are signals of opportunities to forgive. Reframe and retrain your mind to reorient your looking and to recognize the signals. Remember that judgment is a sign of fear. Use your new capacity for sight to see it in yourself. Use your mind to identify it for what it really is.

When you see and know that you have before you an opportunity for forgiveness, then proceed each time in the same way. First apply honesty of mind "to thine own self be true" and look directly at the issue and see there the seeds of harmony that await only your application of forgiveness to bear fruit. Honestly know and then admit that you are not separate from the situation or the brother that has caused your fear and judgment. Acknowledge in your mind that you have not sinned against the Father, that you are guiltless, and that you have been given the gift of seeing this error which is within your power to heal.

Next be sincere in your examination of what you really see, not what the ego wants you to see. Take the images literally and figuratively to heart. Use there the greater sight to let your Spirit sincerely respond with love for both you, the others involved, and the situation. Let the love and wisdom of your heart allow you to make the decision to choose forgiveness. Choose first the forgiveness and then any response that needs to flow from the act of forgiveness.

Should you find especially in the early stages of learning the reframing of your responses to move away from those of the little ego that you have difficulty seeing or choosing, then ask your Holy Spirit to do it for you. Give it to Me, remembering that I am with you always and in all ways.

Lastly, detach from the results of your choice of forgiveness. Whether you have made the decision yourself or given it to Me, release completely to Me both the decision and the manifestation of it.

Then and only then consider and further meditate upon any practical actions assuring that they are only conceptualized within the choice of forgiveness. Do not take it back. Become detachment itself, turn your mind and heart elsewhere, and move on.

I love the way You came full circle to the first exercise.

Love is a great word to use as we come to end this part of the work.

And thus, here is My question of great cosmic significance:

What does the student ask of the hotdog vendor?

Make me One with everything!

Amen!

SOURCES

A Course in Miracles. California: Foundation for Inner Peace, 1976.

Bailey, Alice A. *Ponder on This*, A compilation. New York: Lucis Publishing Company, 1971.

Bailey, Alice A. *The Reappearance of the Christ*. New York: Lucis Publishing Company, 1948.

Borg, Marcus, ed. *Jesus & Buddha, The Parallel Sayings*. California: Seastone, an Imprint of Ulysses Press, 2002.

Calaprice, Alice, ed. *The Quotable Einstein*. New Jersey: Princeton University Press, 1996.

Cedercrans, Lucille. *Creative Thinking*. California: Wisdom Impressions Publishers, 2001.

Cedercrans, Lucille. *The Disciple and Economy*. California: Wisdom Impressions Publishers, 2002.

Crème, Benjamin. *Maitreya's Teachings: The Laws of Life*. USA: Share International Foundation, 2005.

Crème, Benjamin. *Messages from Maitreya the Christ*. California: Tara Center, 1981.

Dyer, Wayne W. *The Power of Intention: Learning to Co-

create Your World Your Way. California: Hay House, Inc., 2004.

Gebser, Jean. *The Ever-Present Origin*. Translation by Noel Barstad with Algis Mickunas. Ohio: Ohio University Press, 1985.

Heider, John. *Tao of Leadership: Lao Tzu's Tao Te Ching Adapted for a New Age*. New York: Bantam Books, 1986.

Holy Bible: King James Version. Illinois: The John A. Dickson Publishing Company, 1929.

Jampolsky, Gerald G., M.D. *Love is Letting Go of Fear*. California: Celestial Arts, 1979.

Jefferson, Thomas. *The Jefferson Bible, The Life and Morals of Jesus of Nazareth*. Massachusetts: Beacon Press, 1989.

Jurriaanse, Aart. *Bridges: Basic Studies in . . . Esoteric Philosophy*. South Africa: Sun Centre, 1978.

Kohn, Alfie. *No Contest—The Case Against Competition*. New York: Houghton Mifflin Company, 1986.

Korten, David C. *The Great Turning, From Empire to Earth Community*. Connecticut: Kumarian Press, Inc. California: Berrett-Koehler Publishers, Inc., 2006.

Krishnamurti, J. *Meditations*. Boston and London: Shambhala, 1991.

Krishnamurti, J. and Dr. David Bohm. *The Ending of Time*. New York: HarperCollins Publishers, 1985.

Renard, Gary R. *The Disappearance of the Universe: Straight Talk About Illusions, Past Lives, Religion, Sex, Politics, and the Miracles of Forgiveness.* California: Hay House, Inc., 2004.

Rifkin, Jeremy. *The Empathic Civilization: The Race to Global Consciousness in a World in Crisis.* New York: Penguin Group, 2009.

Satchidananda, Sri Swami. *The Living Gita: The Complete Bhagavad Gita.* Virginia: Integral ®Yoga Publishers, 1988.

Spong, John Shelby. *The Sins of the Scripture: Exposing the Bible's Texts of Hate to Reveal the God of Love.* New York: HarperCollins Publishers, 2005.

Talbot, Michael. *The Holographic Universe.* New York: HarperCollins Publishers, 1992.

Walsch, Neale Donald. *Conversations with God: an uncommon dialogue, Book 1.* Virginia: Hampton Roads Publishing Company, Inc., 1995.

Washington, James M., ed. *A Testament of Hope: The Essential Writings and Speeches of Martin Luther King Jr.* New York: HarperCollins Publisher, 1986.

Williamson, Marianne. *A Return to Love: Reflections on the Principles of A COURSE IN MIRACLES.* New York: HarperCollins Publishers, 1992.

Yogananda, Paramahansa. *Autobiography of a Yogi.* 11th ed. California: Self-Realization Fellowship, 1987.

LIST OF EXERCISES

Exercise 1   HOW TO SEE

Exercise 2   WHAT YOU SEE IS WHAT YOU GET

Exercise 3   THE GREAT INVOCATION

Exercise 4   A CLEARING EXERCISE FOR WHEN YOU RECOGNIZE THE EMOTIONAL SYMPTOMS OF SEPARATIVE THINKING AND THE UNHOLY STATE OF MIND WHICH HAS RESULTED

Exercise 5   AN EXERCISE WITH WHICH TO BEGIN

Exercise 6   PONDER ON THIS

Exercise 7   PART-TO-WHOLE RECOGNITION

Exercise 8   WOVEN ONENESS

Exercise 9   SEE ALL AND BLESS ALL

Exercise 10   AN ENERGY MOVEMENT AND HEALING VISUALIZATION FOR WHEN YOU ARE READY TO SEE AND THEREBY ASSIST YOUR BROTHER OR SISTER TO SEE THAT THE TWO OF YOU ARE SELF, ONE WITH EACH OTHER AND ONE WITH ALL

Exercise 11   THE SO WHAT QUESTION

Exercise 12   HEALING THROUGH FORGIVENESS

END NOTES

[1] From the song, *Rocky Mountain High*,—John Denver

[2] KJV, Mark 12:28-29

[3] KJV, Luke 11:17

[4] Desiderata, Max Ehrmann

[5] *I Come To The Garden Alone Hymn*

[6] From the song, *All About Soul*,—Billy Joel.

[7] Davy Crockett

[8] KJV, John 10:30

[9] KJV, John 10:34

[10] Shakespeare (Hamlet) and as used thereafter

[11] KJV, John 14:12

[12] KJV, John 14:6

[13] KJV, Acts 17:26

[14] KJV, John 14:6

[15] KJV, Psalms 46:10

[16] Mark Twain

[17] KJV, Mathew 7:7-8

[18] Dr. Martin Luther King Jr., Nobel Speech, 1964

[19] The Great Invocation, Alice A. Bailey

[20] KJV, John 13:34

[21] KVJ, Matthew 10:29

[22] POGO, Walt Kelly

[23] KJV, Matthew 18:22

ON THE COVER

The cover art entitled *Crowned Chakras* is an original color pencil drawing by the scribe of this journal and represents the chakras, major energy centers of the body, as they respond to spiritual energy including that of the Soul